HOW THE
CLINTON CLERGY
CORRUPTED

A PRESIDENT

HE WAS A BRIGHT YOUNG BOY, WHO WALKED A MILE TO CHURCH EVERY SUNDAY, UNTIL MINISTERS TURNED HIM INTO A MORAL TRAGEDY

HOW THE
CLINTON CLERGY
CORRUPTED
A PRESIDENT

MOODY ADAMS

The Olive Press
Publishers

COLUMBIA, SC 29228

ISBN 0–937422–42–88

Published by The Olive Press, a division of Midnight Call Ministries,
West Columbia, SC 29170 U.S.A

Cover Lithography — Simon Froese
Editing by Angie Peters
Books are available in quantity for promotional or premium use. Write to
Director of Special Sales, 4694 Platt Springs Road, West Columbia, SC
29170 for information on discounts and terms or call 803–755–0733.

Printed in the United States of America

For Betty McKay Adams

my devoted wife of 50 years who has
warned me about compromise throughout my life
and worked diligently on this manuscript

The prophets prophesy lies in my name: I sent them not, neither have I commanded them, neither spake unto them: they prophesy unto you a false vision and divination, and a thing of nought, and the deceit of their heart...Thus saith the LORD of hosts, Hearken not unto the words of the prophets that prophesy unto you: they make you vain: they speak a vision of their own heart, and not out of the mouth of the LORD. They say still unto them that despise me, The LORD hath said, Ye shall have peace; and they say unto every one that walketh after the imagination of his own heart, No evil shall come upon you...The prophets prophesy falsely, and the priests bear rule by their means; and my people love to have it so: and what will ye do in the end thereof?
(Jeremiah 14:14, 23:16,17, 5:31).

CONTENTS:

FOREWORD

Moody Adams has challenged us to think about the terrible possibility of Christian clergymen leading others astray by teaching what is not true to the Biblical revelation.

Every Christian, in every age, has to ask—and come to conclusions about—three essential questions regarding heresy: (a) Is heresy possible? (If it is not, it is a waste of time to discuss the matter) (b) Is heresy definable? (Again, if it is not, why bother about the issue?) (c) If heresy is possible and definable, what is the Biblical response to heresy?

Some will disagree with some of the author's conclusions. No conscientious Christian, however, no matter how sanguine, will be comfortable with the thundering silence of the Christian community in the face of blatant heresy on the part of Christian ministers. Nor can we say we did not know, "this thing was not done in a corner!" (Acts 26:26).

Now for a warning: do not be surprised if you conclude this book by solemnly asking yourself "Have I myself been a contributing influence—in any way—on the moral lapse of my president? Or anybody else? Can God depend on me to tell the truth, the whole truth, and nothing but the truth?" you may find yourself asking that even more pointed and truly disconcerting question: "Am I myself guilty of believing or teaching heresy?"

Bill Anderson
Calvary Baptist Church
Clearwater, Florida

INTRODUCTION

This book is not written to defend President Bill Clinton, nor to condemn him. Plenty of writings have done both. The purpose of this book, rather, is to draw something positive out of a very negative chapter in American history; to pinpoint the cause and cure of moral failure.

Throughout 40 years of speaking in over 3,000 church meetings, I have come to know ministers well. Many of them are dedicated men of God devoted to helping people by teaching them the truths of the Bible. But some are deceitful men, interested in subverting the gospel and deceiving their listeners. This fact should not surprise anyone familiar with the Bible. Jesus Christ answered His disciples' request for signs of His return with this admonition: "Take heed that no man deceive you. For many shall come in my name, saying, I am Christ, and shall deceive many....many false prophets shall rise and shall deceive many....there shall arise false christs, and false prophets...insomuch that if it were possible, they shall deceive the very elect" (Matthew 24:4, 5, 11, 24). Note the emphasis on and repetition of the concept of deceit. This is where the President of the United States fits into Bible prophecy. He is a sad product of false, deceitful prophets.

I do not share the pessimism of those who accept defeat by lust and lying as being inevitable and inescapable. This book is written with the confidence that the true gospel of Jesus Christ can lift a person to victory over evil.

I do not possess the nonchalant indifference of those who say, "It doesn't matter. So what if a man commits adultery and lies about it? As long as he continues to do his job well, that is all that matters." Job performance is important. But a key part of a President's job is to set an example to the millions of children who see him as the most admired man in the world.

Nor do I have the despair that cries, "American morals are gone and there is nothing to be done about it. From the president on down, society is dishonest and corrupt. We can't change it." This book is written with the conviction that there is a way for our nation to be reformed. Both history and the Bible teach us that people can be delivered from their passions and a nation rescued from moral decay.

I am not in that group which expects Washington D.C. to stop abortion, pornography, drug abuse and family breakups. Those who do are doomed to extreme disillusionment, as well they should be. Moral reformation must begin in the churches, specifically in the pulpits—not in government. Spiritual decay brought about the nation's moral decay and only a spiritual revival will bring about her healing.

Bill Clinton, a product of a corrupt Christianity, exposes what kind of moral character is produced by deceptive, manipulative ministers. He illustrates how desperately the church needs repentance and revival.

"That the opinion polls reveal an unconcern about behavior that once was more widely considered immoral and unjustifiable is a lesson that our current 'unrighteousness' problem is not and never has been the fault of President

Clinton, but is our fault," says columnist Cal Thomas. "Our lack of concern has produced leaders and a culture that turn a cold shoulder to such things."

Chapter One

WHY DID THE PRESIDENT DO IT?

December 19, 1998 was a day of tragic loss for the United States. Following the House of Representatives' vote to impeach Bill Clinton, the government lost its focus on domestic and international problems. Children lost a moral role model. Bill Clinton lost a historic legacy, his reputation, and many of his friends. Mankind lost some of its hope of rising above its most base passions. God lost a prodigal.

The crucial question is "why?" Why does an intelligent man possess such an adolescent sense of folly? Why did a man destined to gain one of history's great legacies give it all up for such little pleasure? Why did a man of such brilliant political strategy make such misguided moral blunders? Why did the President of the United States, knowing Special Prosecutor Kenneth Starr was tracking every one of his words and deeds with his investigation, engage in repeated, reckless behavior right in the Oval Office?

Dee Dee Myers, President Clinton's press secretary in 1993 and 1994, clearly expressed the nation's shock over Mr. Clinton's affair. "I never believed that Bill Clinton would actually risk his presidency, his job he had studied, dreamed about and prepared for since he was a kid—for something so frivolous, so reckless, so small," she said. "The President's relationship with Monica Lewinsky was so reckless as to seem pathological. He knew the consequences of getting caught, but he went ahead. For 18 months. In the West Wing of the White House." [1]

In the midst of the Clinton scandal, on September 2, 1998, Swissair 111 went down off the coast of Nova Scotia, killing 229 people. Millions of dollars and hundreds of people were dedicated to finding the cause. The public wanted to know so the problem could be corrected and they could gain some confidence that it would not happen again. Likewise, it is important for the public to understand why Clinton crashed morally and what can be done to prevent it from happening again. The important issue is not what the President did, who he did it with, or what his punishment should be. The crucial issue is why he did it. As we probe and search the wreckage of the President's crash to find the answer, we hear a broad array of theories being put forth to explain it.

THE GENETIC THEORY

Geneticists explain that Clinton misbehaved because he was born with "bad genes." He was cursed by having parents whose genes predetermined that he would lie and commit adultery. Jerome D. Levin, a Ph.D. with 25 years of experience treating addictions, wrote in *The Clinton Syndrome*: "Biological influences are found in his maternal grandmother...his biological father...and in his mother." Levin supports this with the fact that Clinton's maternal grandmother was a flirt, a partier, and a gambler who was frequently violent. His father, described as a womanizer, abandoned his wives and possessed "the traits of a con man." Clinton's mother, Levin said, was also a "flirt, a gambler, and a partier."

But a very short search through presidential history demonstrates that "bad genes" do not necessarily determine a person's conduct. President Ronald Reagan was born with similar "bad genes." In *An American Life: Ronald Reagan, the Autobiography*, President Reagan explains that his mother, Nelle Wilson Reagan, waited until he was old enough to understand before telling him his father was an alcoholic. This explained why his daddy was constantly disappearing from home without anyone knowing where he was. His prodigal escapades were marked by bouts of severe drunkerness. Yet, despite his genes, the younger Reagan grew into a man of such character he would not take his coat off in the Oval Office, not to mention his pants.

Even some clergymen are supporting the theory of a "promiscuous gene." The Most Rev. Richard Holloway, an English bishop, says, "Churches should be more understanding when people commit adultery because they have a God-given urge to 'propagate as widely as possible.' God has given us our promiscuous genes so I think it would be wrong for the church to condemn people who have followed their instincts." This Anglican Bishop urges his flock to sow their oats: "For the human race to survive we must go out and sow our seeds." The British paper, *The Guardian*, headlined the Holloway's views: "Bishop Tells Audience to Sow Seed and Scatter." *The Daily Telegraph* chose the headline: "Adultery Not A Sin, Says Bishop."[2]

THE PSYCHOLOGICAL THEORY

Two noted psychiatrists, Dr. Jerome D. Levin, Ph.D., and Dr. Paul Fick, Ph.D., have written books linking President Bill Clinton's fall to psychiatric problems.

Dr. Levin points to the fact that William Jefferson Blythe II, born in Hope, Arkansas on August 19, 1946, was left with his grandparents when he was a year old. His mother, Virginia, left him to go to a school for nurse anesthetists in New Orleans. Levin says, "Virginia's desertion was to have a powerful impact on the infant Bill." The doctor says, "Clinton's compulsive need to have one woman after another continues to be an attempt to reconnect with his mother and to have a more satisfactory relationship with her than he had as a child."[3]

In *Bill Clinton: The Inside Story*, author Robert E. Levin points out what an extremely dysfunctional family the President grew up in. "There were frequent arguments between Virginia and Roger, who was an alcoholic. After drinking, he occasionally beat Virginia. He was usually calm, but when he drank, he became angry. During one episode, he fired a gun into a wall of the living room and was put in jail."

Dr. Paul Fick, Ph.D., says: "We are not observing a man who had an affair and is remorseful for hurting his spouse. We are observing an individual who is consumed with thought and behavior related to sex in much the same way that a drug abuser is consumed with thoughts and behaviors about his compulsion....This is pathological behavior that requires effective treatment."[4]

Fick, in his book *The Dysfunctional President*, writes his diagnosis of President Clinton. "The client is an adult child of an alcoholic stepfather. He adopted the role of hero within the dysfunctional family system. He utilizes denial as a primary defense mechanism. His present behavior and problems indicate that the client has very little insight into the impact of his childhood problems as it relates to his current difficulties. He denies responsibility and blames others. He exhibits periodic outbursts of anger because of the long-standing nature of his pain....It appears that sexually acting out behavior is likely and would be consistent for this individual, given his diagnosis and lack of insight into the problem."[5]

In the *Comeback Kid—The Life and Career of Bill Clinton,* Charles F. Allen and Jonathan Portis say, "He was forced to come to grips with the stormy relationship between his mother and stepfather. Roger Clinton, Sr. was a heavy drinker with a mean streak. He and Virginia had a volatile relationship, frequently separating."

The American Psychiatric Association has a reference book—*The Diagnostic and Statistical Manual*—which is used by professionals in the mental health field to diagnose disorders in their patients. Some of the following criteria it lists for diagnosing sexual addiction apparently fit Mr. Clinton:

1. Having sex in possibly dangerous places.
2. Repeatedly facing legal problems related to sex.
3. Participating in large amounts of sexual conduct that exceed original intentions.
4. Continuing sexual activity in spite of reoccurring problems caused by these activities.

Analyzing the President's sexual addiction, Dr. Jerome Levin says, "Sexual addictions are not about sex. They are about insecurity, low self-esteem, and the need for affirmation and reassurance. The sex addict feels unloved and unlovable and therefore looks obsessively for proof that this is not so."[6]

Psychologists, while not fully absolving Clinton of

responsibility for his conduct, are saying he is largely the victim of a dysfunctional home. And, of course, there is nothing anyone could ever do about that.

A flight attendant announced on a plane going from Baton Rouge to Dallas, "I hope they do find Clinton has a sexual addiction. It would made it easy for us to understand if he was just sick." Evidently, she sees no responsibility for a sick person to seek treatment and stop infecting those around him.

THE 60'S THEORY

Another prevalent theory suggests Clinton is a victim of his generation: he is doomed by having been raised in the "60's." Paul G. Labadie, in a *USA Today* editorial, aptly points out, "Perhaps we should wonder whether anyone from the baby-boomer generation would be able to pass the endoscopic examination of character we so fervently demand of our presidents." Labadie declares Boomers live by the "Gratification Solution: 'I want it all, I want it now, and I'll pick it up at the drive-thru.' Self-discipline is no longer a virtue; it is an anchor, an antiquated sentiment designed to inhibit our ever-expanding comfort zone of inappropriate behavior." Labadie characterizes the thinking of the Clinton generation as: "If we don't have enough money, we simply charge it. If we have marital problems, we simply divorce. If our children's education is inadequate, blame unmotivated teachers and the system. And if we get caught in a compromising situation, cry *victim* and then accuse the accuser."[7]

The 60's generation drastically changed our nation's values. In 1965 only 7.7% of America's children were born out of wedlock. By the mid-1990's, the percentage had soared to 32%.[8] But the 60's did not deprive a generation of its ability to make choices. And the majority chooses not to engage in sex with an employee, in the workplace and then lie to cover it up.

THE ARKANSAS THEORY

"At *Christian Century*, a national magazine for mainstream Protestants, editor James M. Wall first responded (to Clinton's confessed moral failure) with a column titled 'Forgiving and Forgetting,'" says journalist Julia Malone. "In what amounts to an Arkansans-will-be-Arkansans excuse, Wall wrote that 'in that part of the American South where Bill Clinton was born and raised, charming rogues are forgiven for behavior which would destroy anyone else.' Following complaints from readers, Wall reversed both his tone and message two weeks later, with a lament that Americans are taking a 'Who cares?' approach to private behavior in high office. But he continued to withhold judgment on Clinton....Wall acknowledged the dilemma that he shares with many of his theological colleagues. He worked in both of Clinton's presidential campaigns and, along with dozens of the nation's clergy, has been actively courted by Clinton. 'He's not an impersonal leader to me,' Wall said. 'He's someone I know and am concerned about.'"[9]

Wall, in his "Arkansans-will-be-Arkansans" excuse, offers no statistics to substantiate the theory that people in Arkansas commit adultery and lie more often than the folks in Massachusetts or any other state.

THE MALE MENOPAUSE THEORY

Writer Gail Sheehy said on MSNBC that Mr. Clinton is like many men over 50 who try to recapture their youth, thus are very open to temptation. This fits into the theory of male menopause, which explains Clinton's behavior as an aging crisis that has launched him into a search for the youth he has lost. Dorothy Rabinowitz, writing in *The Wall Street Journal*, responded by saying that this is "A strange argument given what we know of Mr. Clinton's behavior thoughout his marriage—from which history we can conclude he has been trying to recapture his youth for the past three decades."[10]

THE PRESIDENTIAL THEORY

Historians have leaped to Clinton's defense by assuring us that presidents throughout history have practiced the "Clinton morality." Nigel Cawthore's book, *Sex Lives of the Presidents From Washington to Clinton,* leads us to believe all the presidents have done it. The book, which substitutes vulgarity for historical accuracy, declares, "The Clinton scandal brought it to the headlines, but presidential promiscuity is as old as the Constitution. It didn't start with Clinton, or even Kennedy. Ever since the Father of our Country was sworn in over 200 years ago, the White House has seen its share of oversexed, adulterous, philandering presidents." The book jacket promises, "From Washington's countless bed partners to Jefferson's illegitimate children, Kennedy's notorious womanizing to Clinton's unstoppable libido, find out the surprising and sometimes bizarre sexual practices of all the men in the Oval Office."

Get that: "All the men" in the White House! In an effort to exonerate Bill Clinton, some are willing to destroy the reputation of every president who has ever served our nation.

These historians of presidential rumors have instilled this theory in many minds: "Clinton's actions simply go with the territory." Eleanor Clift assures us that "libido and leadership" are linked, demanding that we expect the President of the United States to commit adultery.

While there have been a lot of rumors, very few cases of presidential immorality have been proved. The theory that the office of president necessarily destroys the occupant's morals can be countered by the fantastic love letters which flowed from Harry Truman's Oval Office to his beloved Bess back home in Missouri. There was never even a hint of him being unfaithful.

Rather than seeing the office of the presidency as one that destroys morals, some see that office and all public service as a force with potential to lift men to higher morals. George Melloan, writing in *The Wall Street Journal* about the Clinton story, said, "Its tawdry tale was of a commander-in-chief, seemingly devoid of a sense of either honor or duty, engaging in deviant sex in a government office and then lying about it under oath. Everyone who has served in an army knows that soldiers are not angels....But the U.S. military has always tried to give the variegated human animals who serve it something else, a sense of duty, honor and country, a feeling that they are fighting for some higher cause than just the danger and thrill of battle. They are taught that they are defending moral values even as they engage in an activity, killing fellow human beings, that would be considered immoral by most of us if conducted out of personal animus or for personal gain rather than under the banner of patriotic duty."[11]

THE RELIGION THEORY

A theory about the Clinton crash that has received little notice holds that the President's fall was the result of derelict clergymen. The evidence strongly indicates that President Clinton is the finished product of some of the most corrupt teachings ever given in the name of Jesus Christ.

"The greatest crisis of the Clinton presidency is testing the souls of the nation's religious leaders," says journalist Julia Malone. Writing in the *Atlanta Constitution*, Malone says, "How should they deal with allegations of sexual misconduct against a president who is not only a prominent churchgoer, but a personal friend of many in the clergy? Much of the religious community is approaching the subject as if it were a skillet filled with burning oil on a hot stove."

It is appropriate that liberal clergymen should deal with Clinton's fall as a skillet of burning oil. Obviously, the clergymen he has trusted for moral counsel and spiritual instruction have led him astray. There is no denying the tremendous role clergymen have played in shaping Bill Clinton into the moral failure that has shocked the nation.

David Maraniss, Clinton's finest biographer, says, "For Bill Clinton, the prodigal son, religion offered something other than discipline and gratitude and social service. Many clues to the way he has responded to the Lewinsky scandal can be found in his religious history. He began attending church when he was nine years old, toting a leather-bound Bible in his left hand as he walked alone down the streets of Hot Springs, past the motel swimming pools and nightspots parking lots, the corridor of middle-American carefree vacation glitz, to the Park Place Baptist Church."[12]   Rev. Dexter Blevins said Clinton was there every time the door opened. Clinton told Maraniss, "It was moral instruction... trying to get closer to being a good person and understanding what life was all about. I really looked forward to it every Sunday morning, getting dressed up and walking that mile or so alone." Clinton was baptized into a Baptist Church. He served as a member of his church's choir. He carried his Bible and quoted the Scriptures. He counseled with ministers over his major moral decisions. Clinton spent much of his life in church listening to preachers.

Far from being just a nominal church member, Clinton has a well-documented record of respect for ministers and their advice. At age seven, he made a decision during a Billy Graham crusade and at age 12 he started tithing his allowance to the Billy Graham Association. Graham said Clinton's first contribution was ten cents, "And he decided he would give 10 percent of his income to our ministry and our work. And he has told me that he did it for a while."[13]

Clinton has always loved religious music, referring to the song "Holy Ground," which was sung at his mother's funeral, as one of his favorites.[14] Following a political victory celebration at the Excelsior Hotel in Little Rock, Clinton and some friends went to the Governor's mansion. "By eleven, Hillary was tired and ready for bed. Clinton stayed up with a small band of friends who had gathered around Carolyn Staley at the piano. They sang a medley of Mo-town songs, followed by 'Abraham, Martin and John,' the anthem to political martyrs. Clinton sat beside Carolyn on the bench and sang every verse. He knew all the words. Soon the room fell quiet as Carolyn played the opening chords to her friend's favorite hymn. It was approaching midnight on the first day of his campaign for president and William Jefferson Clinton was in full voice. 'A-a-ma-zing grace!' he sang. 'How sweet the sound. That saved a-a wretch like me. I-I once was lost, but now am found. Was blind, but now I see.'"[15]

CLINTON HEARD AND HEEDED
HIS PASTOR'S COUNSEL

Clinton was extremely close to Dr. W. O. Vaught, his pastor in Arkansas. According to Maraniss, "Bill was constantly searching for older male role models: his papaw Eldridge Cassidy, Virgil Spurlin at school, his grandmother's brother Buddy Grisham, his friend Jim Blair, his adviser Maurice Smith, his minister W. O. Vaught."[16] In Rev. Vaught, Clinton found an older role model he trusted.

In addition to being a father figure, Rev. Vaught and Bill Clinton shared a common role. Both were "transitional figures" in battles between fundamentalists and moderates; Clinton in the liberal and conservative political fight, Vaught in the conflict between liberal and conservative factions in the Southern Baptist Convention. Vaught delighted in the way Clinton used the "political equivalent of Biblical language" in an effort to bring about change, and he thought this would take Clinton where he wanted to go.[17]

As Governor of Arkansas, facing his first life-or-death call on a death-row inmate, Clinton invited Vaught for breakfast at the governor's mansion to discuss the death penalty. He had "gone over it a thousand times," Clinton told Vaught. He was facing the issue once again. Maraniss says, "Vaught told Clinton that in the original translations of the Ten Commandments, capital punishment was not prohibited. In ancient Hebrew and Greek, he said, the phrase was 'thou shalt not murder,' not 'thou shalt not kill'—which he said meant it was not the same thing as the laws of the land applying capital punishment." Clinton thanked him for his interpretation because he had "instinctively thought you could make arguments for and against capital punishment, but didn't think it was a violation of Christian faith." Vaught replied, "But you must never worry about whether it's forbidden by the Bible, because it isn't."[18]

When Clinton was confronting the abortion issue, he again turned to his pastor for guidance. Clinton agreed with the pro-choice argument. But he had second thoughts, despite being influenced by the strong pro-choice women surrounding him, including Hillary and Betsey Wright. He wanted Dr. Vaught to give him the Bible's insights on the issue. Vaught said the meaning of life and birth and personhood came from Hebrew words which mean "to breathe life into."[19] He concluded that life does not begin until there is breath; therefore, abortion cannot be murder. Because of this belief, Vaught became a crusader for a woman's right to an abortion. Clinton accepted Vaught's interpretation and concluded there was nothing Biblically wrong with abortion, not even with a partial birth abortion, because those babies have not yet breathed. His trusted pastor's interpretation settled Clinton's pro-abortion stance.

Maraniss said, "During the Lewinsky affair, when Clinton tried to make the argument that oral sex was not sex, he was again, as usual, drawing on his history, and he was basing it not so much on his legal training as on the biblical semantics that he first learned from his Little Rock minister (Dr. W. O. Vaught)."[20]

When Vaught was dying of bone cancer, Clinton stopped by to check on him nearly every week. Once, he brought Billy Graham with him to have prayer. Clinton and some of Vaught's other friends put up a Christmas tree for the dying minister who had been such an influence on him. On Christmas Day, 1989, Rev. Vaught passed away.[21]

IN CLINTON'S DEEPEST CRISIS
HE TURNED TO HIS CLERGYMEN

Time magazine reported, "After the Clinton scandal became public Clinton turned to a minister: the Rev. Jesse Jackson. And though the White House has carefully framed the entire scandal as one immense invasion of privacy....In the middle of the most painful weekend of her life, Hillary invited into her home for comfort the one clergyman in America better known for his pulpit at CNN than at the Fellowship Missionary Baptist Church on Chicago's South Side. It was hard to know what to make of the family's late-night house call by Jesse Jackson....He had been at the White House to watch the Super Bowl back on the first horrible weekend of scandal, and he and Chelsea got along great. It was mainly for her that he was invited back....family friends said, to help talk her out of her funk."[22]

Tragically, after President Clinton's moral weaknesses became public, he selected three liberal ministers to counsel with him. He chose Gordon MacDonald, senior pastor at Grace Chapel in Lexington, Massachusetts, who admitted to an adulterous affair that pushed him out of a previous ministry position; Clinton's Washington pastor, Philip Wogaman, who champions the cause of homosexuals; and his third choice was Tony Campolo, professor of sociology at Eastern College in St. Davids, Pennsylvania who is known to be a man who fights the Bible's teaching on homosexuality and pushes churches to accept perversion. Sending Clinton to these men for counseling is like sending an eight year old to a prison for convicted sex offenders to get advice.

Despite all his religious influence and training, Mr. Clinton grew into a habitual adulterer, a man who deliberately lied and a man who cared for himself more than his family, friends, co-workers, and country. It is easy to understand why Clinton's clergymen are handling the Clinton fall as a skillet filled with burning oil. Their policy of "hands-off, offer a little forgiveness, otherwise keep religion out of it and deny all responsibility for preaching errors that caused the poor man to crash" helps them keep their ministries untarnished.

President Clinton is in about the same shape as King Jehoshaphat when he sought spiritual counseling about going into a battle to capture Ramoth-gilead. Ahab summonsed 400 false prophets who told the King what he wanted to hear, that all would go well. But Jehoshaphat was suspicious and said, "Is there not here a prophet of the LORD besides, that we might inquire of him? And the king of Israel said unto Jehoshaphat, There is yet one man, by whom we may inquire of the LORD: but I hate him; for he never prophesied good unto me, but always evil: the same is Micaiah." Well, Micaiah told him to send his soldiers home or suffer defeat. The king imprisoned Micaiah, the true prophet, went to war on the advice of false prophets, and "about the time of the sun going down he died" (II Chronicles 18:6,7,34).

Instead of a "prophet of the LORD?" Clinton was surrounded by a group like the 400 prophets of Jehoshaphat who told him what he wanted to hear. The "Presidential Prophets" taught Mr. Clinton the most bizarre, anti-Bible truths imaginable. Seeing their teachings will enable us to follow their deception step by step as it brought about the tragedy in which Bill Clinton was a willing player, and his clergymen the coaches.

Chapter Two

MEN OF GOD WHO DID
THE DEVIL'S WORK

Early in his second term, William Jefferson Clinton was awarded his place in history when he became the second president of the United States to be impeached. The entire tragedy could possibly have been averted if the clergymen he had trusted to teach him and train him had done their job. They failed. The President fell. Now it is important for the American people to understand exactly how the Clinton Clergy undermined his life and led him to a moral breakdown.

Imagine the President falling to an assassin's bullet. There would be a relentless investigation of the Secret Service men who guarded him. The public would demand to know if the men responsible for protecting him had done their job properly. Had they been negligent in any way, charges would be brought against these men.

Suppose the President was incapacitated because of

food poisoning. There would be an investigation of the White House staff. We would want to know if they had been careful in the selection, preservation and preparation of Mr. Clinton's food. If evidence indicated they were negligent, charges would be brought against these men.

If the President had fallen from a heart attack, there would be an investigation of his medical records and doctors. Had it been discovered that his doctors knew he had heart disease and had failed to treat him, they would be held responsible. Suppose the President's doctors detected blocked arteries, yet only told the President, "Your stomach is fine; there is not a sign of cancer. Your hearing test is great." This would constitute criminal neglect. But picture a worst-case scenario in which the doctors not only tell him he is fine, but put him on a high-cholesterol diet. This would make the President happy. He would love the doctors who gave him these orders. But he could die as a result.

President Clinton did not fail because of an assassin's bullet, poisoned food or a heart attack. He fell because of lying and adultery. This demands an investigation of the men responsible for his moral and spiritual welfare—his clergymen. Those found negligent should be indicted by an outraged public.

The President had a deep spiritual problem that should have been diagnosed by his ministers. But, it wasn't. They told him he was "a great Christian, a wonderful man, doing a fine job." They ignored the only credible authority of spiritual knowledge, the Bible, and gave their personal opinions instead. They said all Bill Clinton needed was forgiveness. Their advice made Clinton happy. But the result was that he fell into a disgrace worse than death.

If America is to profit at all from this horrid tragedy, it must probe the corrupt counsel given by the President's

Prophets who turned their backs on the Bible they pretend to teach. Bill Clinton is the poster boy of their so-called "liberal Christianity."

Respected Christian researcher George Barna says, "The Christian faith appears to have a minimal influence on the thoughts, words and deeds of people." This is because what is being preached in the majority of churches bears no resemblance at all to the teachings of Jesus Christ. The ministers are called "liberals." Actually, they are cunning clergymen, with the skepticism of atheists, wrapped in ministerial garb.

The President's greatest error was not in getting involved with women who were not his wife. His greatest error was in getting involved with ministers who were not his God's. Jesus Christ wrote to the church of Ephesus: "I know thy works, and thy labour, and thy patience, and how thou canst not bear them which are evil: and thou hast tried them which say they are apostles, and are not, and hast found them liars" (Revelation 2:2). Here is Clinton's grave mistake. He did not take his Bible and try, or test those who said they were men of God. Had he done so, he would have found many of them were "liars."

Clinton, the super seducer, was himself seduced— seduced by his clergymen. The Bible warns of this: "Be mindful of the words which were spoken before by the holy prophets, and of the commandment of us the apostles of the Lord and Savior....These things have I written unto you concerning them that seduce you" (I John 2:26-29). By taking heed to the Scriptures, Clinton could have found out his clergymen were seducing him.

Newsweek religion correspondent Kenneth L. Woodward jumped on the influence of the Clinton Clergy in corrupting the President. In *Newsweek*, November 2, he says, "To understand Clinton the president, you have to meet Bill the Baptist, a believer whose faith leaves plenty of license." In an article that drew 200 E-mail responses (more than the cover story), Woodward theorizes that the Baptist doctrine of "soul competency," or the believer's right to interpret scripture for himself, combined with "once saved, always saved," could be interpreted as a license to sin.

"Clinton's troubled personal life—and his repeated verbal evasions—also bears a distinctive Baptist stamp. Like most Baptists, Clinton was taught that because he had been born again, his salvation is ensured. Sinning—even repeatedly—would not bar his soul from heaven," says Woodward.

Responding to the "soul competency" charges, historian E. Glenn Hinson of Baptist Theological Seminary in Richmond, Va., said, "As a born-again Baptist, however, the President believes that what he does in private is nobody's business but the Lord's. Woodward commented, "When the president told the nation that his problems were between himself, his family and 'our God,' that was a very Baptist statement."

Woodward's mistake in this controversial article was he didn't explain the difference between these Biblically based doctrines and the perverted interpretation some like the President's Prophets gave them. The believer can interpret scripture for himself, but he cannot choose to believe scriptures about God's forgiveness and ignore Scriptures demanding repentance. Neither is he free to twist Scriptures out of their Biblical context. Regarding "once saved, always saved," it is not a license to sin when you understand what you are saved from, sin, not just the consequences of sin. The continual practice of sin does not indicate a person has lost their salvation, but rather that they never had it.

President Clinton is not off the hook. But his ministers

are certainly on that hook. There is irrefutable proof that the Clinton Clergy have a grave responsibility for the moral fall of the President. These ministers face three indictments.

INDICTMENT 1:
FAILING TO SET CLINTON FREE
FROM DESTRUCTIVE PASSIONS

First, the Clinton Clergy never freed him from his passions. Jesus Christ promised, "And ye shall know the truth, and the truth shall make you free" (John 8:32). The meaning of these words is inescapable. Mr. Clinton was not set free of his passions because he did not know the truth. His clergymen did not tell it to him. They told him lies. If a man hears the truth and will not accept it, then he must bear the responsibility. But if a man does not hear the truth from his clergymen, then the clergymen must share the responsibility.

The Bible declares Christ came to liberate the captives of sin, like Bill Clinton, from their lust: "The Spirit of the Lord GOD is upon me; because the LORD hath anointed me to preach good tidings unto the meek; he hath sent me to bind up the brokenhearted, to proclaim liberty to the captives, and the opening of the prison to them that are bound" (Isaiah 61:1). But Clinton was not liberated from his lusts. Scripture promises to make new people out of sinners: "Therefore if any man be in Christ, he is a new creature: old things are passed away; behold, all things are become new" (II Corinthians 5:17). Clinton was not made into a new, Christ-like man. So what are we to believe? Are the promises of the Bible mere fables? Is the Holy Spirit a fantasy without the power to deliver a man from sexual temptations? Or is Clinton the product of ministers who are preaching a false gospel? The evidence points to the latter.

• Clinton's Arkansas pastor, Dr. W. O. Vaught, has taught

him he does not have to repent of lying and adultery.

- Clinton's Washington pastor, Dr. Philip Wogaman, has said the Bible is like *The Washington Post*, in that it contains both truth and errors.

- Bishop Spong, speaking in Clinton's Washington church has declared, "The resurrection and virgin birth of Jesus did not actually happen....the Ten Commandments (are) immoral....the apostle Paul was a homosexual....a self-hating, gay man."

- Members of the Clinton Clergy have taught him that as long as he believes there is a "god" somewhere out there, he is "saved."

- His pastor has said straight sex is a sin, but oral sex is okay.

- Clinton has been told that everyone has a God-given obligation to forgive him and demand no punishment, regardless of whether or not he confesses his misconduct, or quits engaging in it.

- Presidential Prophets have emphasized that we are all morally equal: "No one is perfect, so Clinton should not expect to live free of fornicating and lying."

- Ministers have taught the President that anyone who offers correction is casting stones at him and is, therefore, un-Christian.

- Clinton's preachers have stressed that as long as he does his job well, sinning is secondary.

- The President's Prophets have been careful not to mention Hell, the need to be born again, or Jesus' instruction that if a part of your body causes you to sin, "cut it off."

- Clinton's clergymen have not only perverted the truth of God, they have also led people in the worship of false gods. Clinton's Founders Methodist Church in Washington held a women's conference in which the Greek earth goddess Gaia was asked for a blessing. And in 1993, the United Methodist, Presbyterian, Lutheran and American Baptist churches "featured a veneration of 'Sophia, Creator God'...and rites from other religions such as the American Indian tobacco ritual."[23]

The prophet Jeremiah indicted this type of false clergymen and the people who tolerated them: "An astonishing and horrible thing has been committed in the land: The prophets prophesy falsely, and the priests rule by their own power; and My people love to have it so" (Jeremiah 5:30,31). Joseph Parker, like a modern Jeremiah, indicts both the false prophets of today and the churches who tolerate them: "They do not prize Scriptural teaching. They want to hear something fresh, racy, piquant, startling. They do not sit, Bible in hand, testing the speaker by the revelation; and what they ask for they get. They ask for chaff, and they get it."[24]

Outstanding Christian teacher Warren W. Wiersbe points out the tragic results of such counterfeit Christianity: "The weakness of the church helped to cause these scandals. The church is the salt of the earth, but apparently we are not salty enough to hinder corruption in government, big business, sports, or even religious ministry. The church is the light of the world, but that light is apparently too weak to have much of an influence on today's movers and shakers."[25]

Jesus Christ made a stinging indictment of men who do not preach the truth, calling them "false:" "For there shall arise false christs, and false prophets" (Matthew 24:24). He warns us not to be deceived by them: "Beware of false prophets, which come to you in sheep's clothing, but inwardly they are ravening wolves. Ye shall know them by their fruits" (Matthew 7:15,16). Christ marked these men so we can recognize them. They are distinguished by teaching man's words instead of God's: "But in vain they do worship me, teaching for doctrines the commandments of men" (Matthew 15:9). Jesus foretold these false teachers will lead men to a disastrous fall: "They be blind leaders of the blind. And if the blind lead the blind, both shall fall into the ditch" (Matthew 15:14). Bill Clinton is a living fulfillment of this prophecy. He followed blind ministers and he ended up in a very deep, humiliating ditch.

INDICTMENT 2:
PREACHERS MADE CLINTON FEEL COMFORTABLE WHILE LIVING IN SIN

The President's prophets have not only failed to deliver Clinton from the bondage of his sins, but they haven't even preached enough truth in make him uncomfortable. When Jesus Christ was on earth, His plain, straightforward words struck terror in the hearts of men. Some repented and became His disciples. Those who didn't could not stand to keep listening to Christ. One day, after Christ preached a very demanding message... "many of his disciples went back, and walked no more with him. Then said Jesus unto the twelve, Will ye also go away?" (John 6:66,67). Judas stayed the longest of any unconverted man. After three years, he couldn't take it any more, and left. What a contrast between the preaching of Jesus Christ and that of the Presidential Prophets.

Cebe Bradham, a powerful country preacher who built effective churches in the towns of Clinton and Jackson, Louisiana, stirred his area for Christ, and delivered many out of wicked lives. He declared, "If you preach the Word of God people will either get right or get out." The Bible certainly supports this. Instead of driving Mr. Clinton to either get right or get out of the church, the President's clergy have comforted him, praised him and kept him very comfortable while he has been living in flagrant sin.

Rev. Dr. Joan Brown Campbell, general secretary of the National Council of Churches, once had a "laying on of hands" ceremony for Clinton—as if he was a missionary departing to spread the Gospel in Africa. "When Christians have their backs to the wall, they pray," Campbell told Clinton, standing before him with the 14 other clerics she'd brought with her. "One of the most powerful forms of Christian prayer is expressed in the laying on of hands, a practice more common to African-American and Pentecostal denominations than to white, mainline Protestant churches. After describing this ancient form of ministry, Campbell asked the leader of the Free World if he'd consent. And so, right there in the Oval Office, with 30 hands touching the presidential shoulders, Bishop Nathaniel Linsey of the Christian Methodist Episcopal Church asked God to 'make the president strong for the task' of protecting society's most vulnerable. Clinton was moved to weep."[26]

On *Larry King Live*, Billy Graham declared how wonderful the Clintons are: "My feelings are that I love him as a personal friend, a very close personal friend...but 'if' he was guilty of some of these things, I would be disappointed." King asked, "That's 'if.' We have to say if.' You would be disappointed." Graham responded, "Yes, 'if,' because it's all allegations. There's no proof that I have seen." Then Larry King asked, "How do you assess the way Hillary has handled all this?" Rev. Graham answered, "Oh, without her, I don't think he would have made it in many, many periods in his life. She is an amazing woman." King then asked, "You know her so well. What's so special about her?" Graham explained, "I think her intellect and her tremendous training. She was raised in a strong Methodist church near Chicago, and she has strong, deep religious and moral feelings of herself that people don't know about, but she does. She wrote me a letter last week, a handwritten letter, and sent me a little picture of the two of us taken together at dedication of the Bush library in Texas. And she wrote a little handwritten note that was very personal, and I appreciated it. She's very thoughtful to her friends and I think a great deal of her, but I think that he has real difficulties with certain things in his life, and I think he needs a lot of prayer and a lot of love and a lot of understanding." Such words may be appropriate and comforting. But they will not disturb sinners to get right or get out.

Jesus Christ said that people living in sin hate the light of the true gospel: "This is the condemnation, that light is come into the world, and men loved darkness rather than light, because their deeds were evil. For every one that doeth evil hateth the light, neither cometh to the light, lest his deeds should be reproved. But he that doeth truth cometh to the light, that his deeds may be made manifest, that they are wrought in God" (John 3:19-21). There was no such hated light in the praise-the-President preaching Clinton has listened to from his hand picked clergymen.

The life of John the Baptist is a stinging indictment against the Clinton Clergymen. He got his head cut off for faithfully confronting King Herod with his sexual misconduct. Bill Clinton has spent his public life surrounded by preachers who have failed to ever trouble him enough to leave the church, much less who have wanted to kill him. Christ said John the Baptist was "great in the sight of God." Imagine where the President's Prophets stand "in the sight of God."

The life and teachings of the Apostle Paul are forceful charges against the Clinton Clergy. He said he was not in the ministry to gain popularity, money or glory by flattering people: "Our exhortation was not of deceit....But as we were allowed of God to be put in trust with the gospel, even so we speak; not as pleasing men, but God, which trieth our hearts.

For neither at any time used we flattering words, as ye know, nor a cloak of covetousness; God is witness: Nor of men sought we glory" (I Thessalonians 2:3-6). Paul condemns flattering preachers as corrupters: "For we are not as many, which corrupt the word of God: but as of sincerity, but as of God, in the sight of God speak we in Christ" (II Corinthians 2:17).

Theologian Bernard M. G. Reardon has denounced compromised churches for doing little more than echoing the surrounding culture rather than challenging it. Reeves says, "Liberal Protestantism ... has succeeded in making itself dispensable."[27] After looking at what Clinton's churches have contributed to his spiritual development, they certainly appear dispensable. If any purpose is served by churches which do not preach the truth, it is tickling the ears of the ungodly and affording them a pleasant feeling: "But evil men and seducers shall wax worse and worse, deceiving, and being deceived....For the time will come when they will not endure sound doctrine; but after their own lusts shall they heap to themselves teachers, having itching ears; And they shall turn away their ears from the truth, and shall be turned unto fables" (II Timothy 3:13, 4:3,4).

George Whitfield, the revivalist who shook his world, said: "As God can send a nation or people no greater blessing than to give them faithful, sincere, and upright ministers, so the greatest curse that God can possibly send upon a people in this world is to give them over to blind, unregenerate, carnal, lukewarm, and unskilled guides. And yet, in all ages we find that there have been many wolves in sheep's clothing....that prophesied smoother things than God did allow."[28]

The great Bible teacher, Dr. A. J. Gordon, indicts those who preach a "popular Jesus" and present only the joy of salvation. In his sermon on "The Repulsions of Christianity,"

Gordon said: "We dwell much upon the attractions of Christianity, but rarely stop to think that it may also have repulsions which are vitally necessary to its purity and permanence. If the Church of Christ draws to herself that which she cannot assimilate to herself, her life is at once imperiled; for the body of believers must be at one with itself, though it be at war with the world. Its purity and its power depend, first of all, upon its unity. So that if perchance the Church shall attract men without at the same time transforming them; if she shall attach them to her membership without assimilating them to her life—she has only weakened herself by her increase, and diminished herself by her additions." Throughout his life, Mr. Clinton has found no revulsion in the churches he has attended. He has sat comfortably in church while living in sin. He has been "attached" to the church, but not "assimilated" into the life of the church.

In the tiny South Louisiana town of Ethel where I once lived, there was a great black minister named Rev. Boston Jackson. One morning when he stopped at Pete Hall's service station to get gas, Pete asked him how things were at his church. "Mister Pete, things are in mighty bad shape at the church." Pete, expressing dismay, said, "I thought things were going good. You have a mighty nice new auditorium. Are you having financial problems or some kind of disagreement in the membership?" Jackson replied, "No sir. Finances are good and there is no quarreling."

"Well what is wrong?" asked Pete. "That's what's bothering me," Rev. Jackson said. "I don't know Mister Pete. But, I know something is wrong. Jesus done preached this gospel three years and they nailed Him to a cross. I been preaching to this bunch for 30 years and they ain't laid a hand on me. Something has got to be terribly wrong." The Clinton catastrophe tells us something must be terribly wrong in the churches which have raised him, shaped him and tried to shield him from the consequences of his actions.

David Klinghoffer, literary editor at *National Review*, reviewed Thomas Reeves' book, *The Empty Church: The Suicide of Liberal Christianity*. He writes, "Mr. Reeves lays out the facts with clarity and obvious passion. Since the 1960s and '70s, the mainline denominations have bled between a fifth and a third of their congregants. In our 'post-Christian' era, they maintain, old-fashioned Christianity repels potential churchgoers. The solution is to follow the descending path of modern culture to whatever depths it leads."[29] Where it leads is to the graveyard of fallen souls, to the cemetery of Clinton.

INDICTMENT 3:
CLINTON'S CHURCH FAILED TO
CARRY OUT ITS GOD-GIVEN PLAN

Throughout all the years of charges about Mr. Clinton's misconduct, his church in Little Rock, Arkansas, has totally ignored the Bible's plan for restoring an erring member. R. Albert Mohler, Jr., President of the Southern Baptist Theological Seminary in Louisville, Kentucky, puts the blame for Clinton's fall squarely on the shoulders of Immanuel Baptist Church in Little Rock. Clinton has, Mohler contends, "continued attending church while living in sin only "Because the congregation which holds his membership has failed to exercise any semblance of church discipline."[30]

The Bible places a responsibility on Christians when a member of their church is involved in misconduct: "Brethren, if a man be overtaken in a fault, ye which are spiritual, restore such an one in the spirit of meekness; considering thyself, lest thou also be tempted" (Galatians 6:1). Christians are to take an humble, meek approach to helping someone in trouble. But they have a prescribed course of action. The Bible requires them to pray, confront, rebuke, and take the matter before the church. When all else fails to prompt the straying members to repentance, they are to put the person out of the church.

It is unthinkable that the government is following a man-made constitution in dealing with the President's moral failure, but the church is completely ignoring its God-given constitution—the Bible—in handling Clinton's sins. Under the heading, *Irrelevant church*?, Larry E. Ball writes, "In all the discussion of the sins of President Clinton, there is sadly one missing element that even Christian journalists and American pop preachers have failed to grasp...Where is President Clinton's church in all this? No wonder the church is considered irrelevant in America!"[31]

THE MOTIVE OF MINISTERS
WHO FAIL TO FOLLOW THEIR BIBLES

Why don't preachers tell the truth, the truth of the Bible? Cal Thomas, a conservative columnist said, "In the 1980s, a lot of preachers were compromised because they preferred access to accountability. The White House is a powerful seduction, spurring people to pull their punches and avoid saying what they should say. But they deceive themselves if they believe there is a higher purpose to be achieved in communing with the president."[32]

The Apostle Peter foretold how unfaithful preachers would turn people like Bill Clinton into mere merchandise for their own profit: "But there were false prophets also among the people, even as there shall be false teachers among you, who privily shall bring in damnable heresies, even denying the Lord that bought them, and bring upon themselves swift destruction. And many shall follow their pernicious ways; by reason of whom the way of truth shall be evil spoken of. And through covetousness shall they with feigned words make merchandise of you: whose judgment now of a long time lingereth not, and their damnation slumbereth not" (II Peter 2:1-3).

In 1953, Rev. Bill Allen told me there are two kinds of preachers: some who are using people to build great churches, and others who are using the churches to build great people. Here is the big question for ministers, "Are you a preacher who will tell people anything they want to hear in order to build you a great church? Or are you willing to hold up Bible truths in order to help people, even though it costs you and your church ? For the Clinton Clergy, the answer is they have been using him to gain political favor, influence, and publicity so they could build "a greater, more prestigious church."

While Clinton has been accused of forming policy by public polls, the Presidential Prophets have done worse. They have written their sermons by public polls, telling the people it was the Word of God. This approach may gain the favor of some wealthy members, but it is not gaining the favor of heaven. Compromised preaching may be winning political recognition, but it is not winning the souls of men.

How can men stand in the pulpit and pour out deceitful lies about God and manage to live with themselves? The Bible says that their consciences have been seared, or deadened: "the Spirit speaketh expressly (plainly), that in the latter times some shall depart from the faith, giving heed to seducing spirits, and doctrines of devils; Speaking lies in hypocrisy; having their conscience seared with a hot iron" (I Timothy 4:1-2).

The Bible declares Christians should have zero tolerance for clergymen whose motives are anything other than to proclaim the Word of God. Scripture calls for a curse on them: "I marvel that ye are so soon removed from him that called you into the grace of Christ unto another gospel: Which is not another; but there be some that trouble you, and would pervert the gospel of Christ. But though we, or an angel from heaven, preach any other gospel unto you than that which we have preached unto you, let him be accursed. As we said before, so say I now again, If any man preach any other gospel unto you than that ye have received, let him be accursed" (Galatians 1:6-8).

What would have happened if Bill Clinton's pastor had nourished him in the Bible as the Apostle Paul did his congregation? He said: "But we were gentle among you, even as a nurse cherisheth her children: So being affectionately desirous of you, we were willing to have imparted unto you, not the gospel of God only, but also our own souls, because ye were dear unto us" (I Thessalonians 2:7-8). It is sad that Bill Clinton could not have been raised in a church with a pastor like Paul. Such a minister would have passionately worked to develop him into a strong, Christ-like Christian. "And this I say, lest any man should beguile you with enticing words. For though I be absent in the flesh, yet am I with you in the spirit, joying and beholding your order, and the steadfastness of your faith in Christ. As ye have therefore received Christ Jesus the Lord, so walk ye in him: Rooted and built up in him, and stablished in the faith, as ye have been taught, abounding therein with thanksgiving. Beware lest any man spoil you through philosophy and vain deceit, after the tradition of men, after the rudiments of the world, and not after Christ" (Colossians 2:4-8).

Paul constantly warns us against the kind of preachers that have corrupted Clinton. He admonishes Christians to grow up, wise up, and see how cunningly false preachers are working to deceive the Clintons of this world: "That we henceforth be no more children, tossed to and fro, and carried about with every wind of doctrine, by the sleight of men, and cunning craftiness, whereby they lie in wait to deceive" (Ephesians 4:14).

For Americans to maintain their political freedom, they must learn the Constitution and make war against those who would subvert it. To maintain freedom from the evil passions that assail them, they must learn the Bible and fight against those who would subvert it.

BILL CLINTON'S BEST SERMON

Two men have suggested Bill Clinton enter the Christian ministry. One was a Jesuit named Otto Hentz, who taught Clinton introductory philosophy at Georgetown. Assuming Clinton was a Catholic, he said, "'I think you should seriously consider becoming a Jesuit...I've been impressed with your papers." An amused Clinton asked, "Don't you think I oughta become a Catholic first?" "You're not?" Hentz replied. "No, I'm not. I'm a Southern Baptist." A surprised Hentz commented, "I saw all the Jesuits traits in him—serious, political, empathetic. I just assumed he was Catholic."[33]

The other suggestion came from Dr. Billy Graham, who said he hoped Bill Clinton would become an evangelist after his political career was over. He explained that the President meets all of the qualifications.[34] Perhaps Bill Clinton has done exactly that—become an evangelist. By his life, Clinton may be delivering the most powerful sermon this generation will hear. His life is loudly preaching this message to billions: "Compromised Christianity doesn't work. Trusting ministers who do not trust the Bible can destroy you. A corrupt gospel produces corrupt character."

The time has come for every true Christian to stand up and indict the false clergymen who betray the trusting souls who come to hear God's Word—who betray the Bill Clintons of today's world.

Chapter Three

"ALL THIS AND HEAVEN TOO!"

The President's Prophets drove a stake through Bill Clinton's heart in teaching him that he does not have to turn from his sins to be a Christian. As shocking as it sounds, Clinton's pastor has said he does not have to give up adultery, lying, or any other sin. He assured Clinton that he can commit all the sins he wants and still wind up in heaven. Convinced that he does not have to repent, the President hasn't repented. As a result, his sins have wrecked him and produced a historic tragedy.

Rev. W. O. Vaught made a real issue of the fallacy that people do not have to repent of their sins. In his book, *Believe Plus Nothing*, Dr. Vaught said, "For a good many years I have had the conviction that the most misunderstood doctrine of Christianity is the doctrine of salvation. What does a man have to do in order to be saved? The answer most often given goes something like this: 'Repent of your sins and believe in Christ.' This answer is given with the idea that if the unsaved person will be sorry for his sins, turn from his sins, turn over a new leaf (some even say, 'You have been walking in one direction, now turn and walk in the opposite direction'), then if you will believe in Christ, you will be saved.' In some ways, the doctrinal emphasis of this book challenges that idea and demonstrates from Scripture that the unbeliever must only do one thing to be saved, and that one thing is to believe in Jesus Christ."[35]

Clinton's Arkansas pastor was once a man of sounder beliefs. But later in life he came under the influence of Robert Thieme, a teacher known for strange interpretations of the Bible. Dr. Vaught introduced a book by saying: "I am indebted to the doctrinal teaching found recorded in the tapes of R. B. Thieme, Jr., of Houston, Texas, who is one of the leading Greek and Hebrew scholars of our time." Thieme's teaching led Vaught to this startling position: "When we go out to win men to Christ, we should never mention sins. We should only mention Christ. For the unsaved man, sins are not the issue; Christ is the issue."[36]

VAUGHT DECLARED WAR ON REPENTANCE

Rev. Vaught emphatically taught Bill Clinton he does not have to give up his sins. He even taught Clinton it is not possible for him to abandon his sins: "No unsaved man can repent of his sins. If he could repent of one sin, then he could repent of all of his sins, and if he could do this there would be no reason for Him to go to the cross and be saved.....If Christ handled all our sins on the cross, and He did, we can do nothing concerning our sins, for Christ has already done it all," said Vaught. "Therefore, repentance for the unsaved man is beamed toward Christ, not toward sins."[37]

Vaught encouraged his listeners to forget about repenting of adultery, lying, etc., and focus on just one sin unbelief. "The issue of salvation concerns one sin and one sin only, and that is the sin of unbelief. Therefore, sins are not the issue in salvation. Sin, the sin of unbelief, is the issue," he writes.[38]

In his war against repentance of sin, Vaught even assailed one of Christendom's most beloved hymns, *Victory in Jesus*: "In some of our songbooks there is a very beautiful song written by E. M. Bartlett of Arkansas. It is a very lovely song because it reminds us of the victory Jesus brings into the life of the believer. However, the theology of the first verse in the song is inaccurate. Let me quote the words:

'I heard an old, old story,
How a Saviour came from glory,
How he gave his life on Calvary
To save a wretch like me:
I heard about his groaning,
Of his precious blood's atoning,
Then I repented of my sins
And won the victory.'

I think I understand what the writer was trying to say, but the theology is incorrect. At my salvation I did not do something that won the victory..... I believe the greatest truth included in the message of salvation is *Believe, Plus Nothing*."[39]

The pastor of Immanuel Baptist Church hammered his point: "The unsaved man can repent of only one sin, and that is the sin of unbelief. After salvation, the saved man repents of sins by means of confession."[40] What the Bible actually says is, "God is light, and in him is no darkness at all. If we say that we have fellowship with him, and walk in darkness, we lie, and do not the truth: but if we walk in the light, as he is in the light, we have fellowship one with another, and the blood of Jesus Christ his son cleanseth us from all sin" (I John 1:5-7). The promise of cleansing from sin is only given to those who turn from their "walk in darkness" to "walk in the light." This is repentance.

Vaught's teaching assured the man who was destined to be President that he does not have to change his behavior. All he has to do is say, "Well, God, I have gone and sinned again," and *ZAP!* God cleanses his sins. Pastor Vaught said, "I John 1:9 says that if we confess, acknowledge, recognize the sin God will forgive it."[41] Vaught fails to mention that in this verse, John uses the pronoun "we," limiting this promise to Christians who are walking in the light of God's truth.

The subtitle of Vaught's book, *Believe Plus Nothing,* viciously attacks his fellow ministers who preach repentance, declaring the book is "an answer to apostasy." By choosing the extremely harsh word "apostasy," Clinton's pastor declared these fellow ministers apostates, or false prophets preaching a false gospel.

THEY TWISTED THE
MEANING OF REPENTANCE

If Bill Clinton were to sit down and read what the Bible says about repentance, he might well feel like the most betrayed man in Washington. He would be shocked at how preachers around him have misrepresented the Bible. The Scripture makes it abundantly clear that people have to turn away from their sins, but the President's clergyman has made no such demand.

In Thayer's Greek lexicon, *"metanoia,"* the Greek word translated "repent," is defined as "the change of mind of those who have begun to abhor their errors and misdeeds, and have determined to enter upon a better course of life, so that it embraces both a recognition of sin and sorrow for it and hearty amendment, the tokens and effects of which are good deeds."[42]

The Apostle Paul complemented the Christians in Thessalonica saying, they "were examples to all that believe in Macedonia and Achaia....in every place your faith to God-ward is spread abroad....ye turned to God from idols to serve the living and true God" (I Thessalonians 1:9). Paul bragged on them for they "turned to God from idols." It is impossible to turn to God without turning away from sin. The word for that turning is repentance.

The great Bible expositor D. Martyn Lloyd-Jones said what Rev. Vaught should have told Clinton, "Repentance means that you realize that you are a guilty, vile sinner in the presence of God, that you deserve the wrath and punishment of God, that you are hell-bound. It means that you begin to realize that this thing called sin is in you, that you long to get rid of it, and that you turn your back on it in every shape and form. You renounce the world whatever the cost, the world in its mind and outlook as well as its practice, and you deny yourself, and take up the cross and go after Christ. Your nearest and dearest, and the whole world, may call you a fool, or say you have religious mania. You may have to suffer financially, but it makes no difference. That is repentance."[43]

The Apostle Paul and Barnabas demanded that people turn from their sins. When people were about to offer an idolatrous sacrifice, "they rent their clothes, and ran in among the people, crying out, And saying, Sirs, why do ye these things? We also are men of like passions with you, and preach unto you that ye should turn from these vanities unto the living God, which made heaven, and earth, and the sea, and all things that are therein" (Acts 14:14,15). These men of God demanded that they turn from their vain sins, "unto the living God."

Paul explained how the Christians at Thessalonica were converted: "You turned to God from idols to serve the living and true God" (I Thessalonians 1:9). They repented of their idol worship and turned their affections to the Lord Jesus Christ.

When Paul stood before King Agrippa, he recounted his call to preach: "And I said, Who art thou, Lord? And he said, I am Jesus whom thou persecutest....I have appeared unto thee for this purpose, to make thee a minister and a witness both of these things which thou hast seen, and of those things in the which I will appear to open their eyes, and to turn them from darkness to light, and from the power of Satan unto God, that they may receive forgiveness of sins, and inheritance among them which are sanctified by faith that is in me. Whereupon, O king Agrippa, I was not disobedient unto the heavenly vision" (Acts 26:15,16,18,19). If Clinton's Clergymen had not been disobedient to this vision, they would have been telling him he must "turn...from darkness to light" and turn from the "power of Satan unto God."

Paul put his life on the line in order to tell people, "that they should repent and turn to God, and For these causes the Jews caught me in the temple, and went about to kill me" (Acts 26:20,21). Obviously, repentance is more than just a "turn to God;" it is a turn *from* the power of Satan.

Repentance is as much a part of the foundation of a Christian's life as faith: "Therefore leaving the principles of the doctrine of Christ, let us go on unto perfection; not laying again the foundation of repentance from dead works, and of faith toward God" (Hebrews 6:1).

The Jewish prophet Ezekiel made it extremely clear that repentance means to turn "from all your abominations:" "Thus saith the Lord GOD; Repent, and turn yourselves from your idols; and turn away your faces from all your abominations" (Ezekiel 14:6).

Even the Bible passage most often quoted by politicians says God does not forgive people's sins until after they have "turned from their wicked ways": "If my people, which are called by my name, shall humble themselves, and pray, and seek my face, and turn from their wicked ways: then will I hear from heaven, and will forgive their sins, and will heal their land" (II Chronicles 7:14).

VAUGHT DECLARED THOSE WHO PREACH REPENTANCE HAVE ABANDONED THE FAITH

Yet Clinton's pastor, W. O. Vaught, charged these Bible preachers and the majority of his fellow Baptist ministers with driving people away from Christ. "Countless millions have been driven away from Christianity because so-called sincere and devoted soul-winners have gone out to witness and have made sins the issue," he declared.[44] This ignores the fact that God made sins the issue for 2,000 years before Christ died for our sins. He gave the law at Sinai and waited two millennia to send Christ to die for mankind's sins at Calvary. The cross means nothing to people who are not convicted of their sinfulness.

Bill Clinton found it easy to believe his pastor, who was loved throughout Arkansas and around the nation. Through television, he amassed a large following of people who trusted him and who, in fact, ordered over two million of his preaching tapes. Besides this, Vaught was a national leader in America's largest Protestant denomination, the Southern Baptist Convention. A graduate of the largest Southern Baptist seminary, in Louisville, Kentucky, he was president of the Southern Baptist Pastor's Conference in 1960 and first vice-president of the Southern Baptist Convention in 1961. In 1974 he was elected President of the Foreign Mission Board of the Southern Baptist Convention and from 1945 to 1983 he pastored Immanuel Baptist Church in Little Rock, where Clinton remains a member. When Vaught told Bill Clinton he does not have to repent of his sins, he had every reason to believe this is the correct truth of the Bible, despite how wrong it is.

THE INFLUENCE OF THIS TEACHING
ON CLINTON AND HIS STAFF

President Clinton demonstrated he believed in Christ by word and action, though he did not repent of his sins. He gave his personal testimony of faith in Jesus Christ at a Presidential Prayer Breakfast and when the Post Office decided to cancel the popular Madonna and Child stamp because it seemed too religious for Christmas, President Clinton intervened to bring it back.[45] These were brave actions, worthy of praise and evidence he believes. The missing element is a turning from sin, or repentance.

Clinton's problems are common to all men. Our love for sin is rooted in our nature. But this can be eliminated by the power of God and a clear understanding of repentance, an understanding the President has evidently never had. One of history's great Bible teachers, Arthur W. Pink, explained men cannot genuinely believe in Christ and be saved from the curse of their evil nature until they first repent of sin: "Since it be true that the roots of...licentiousness are found in every man by nature....The trumpet he (the preacher) is called upon to blow must give forth no uncertain sound at this point; nothing but faith in the finished work of Christ, and nothing added thereto, can supply the sinner with a standing-ground before the thrice Holy God. On the other hand....unless he makes it as plain as an object bathed in the light of a noonday sun that God hates sin, all sin, and will not compromise with, nor condone it in anyone; unless he declares and insists that Christ came to save His people from their sins—from the love of them, from the dominion of them—he has failed at the most essential part of his task. The great work of the evangelist is to press the authoritative claims of the Creator and Judge of all the earth, to show how short we have come of meeting God's just require-ments, to announce His imperative demand of repentance—the sinner must throw down the weapons of his rebellion and forsake his evil way before he can trust in Christ to the saving of his soul."

Fifty years before President Clinton's fall, another of America's great Bible teachers predicted it. Dr. Harry Iron-sides said, "Shallow preaching that does not grapple with the terrible fact of man's sinfulness and guilt, calling on 'all men everywhere to repent,' results in shallow conversions; and so we have myriads of glib-tongued professors today who give no evidence of regeneration whatever. Prating of salvation by grace, they manifest no grace in their lives."[46] Bill Clinton's pastor preached sermons that did not grapple with "the terrible fact of man's sinfulness and guilt." The predicted result is obvious. President Clinton is a friendly, likable man who produces "no evidence of regeneration whatever."

When President Clinton got around to using the "r" word—repentance—at a September, 1998 prayer breakfast, it appeared a little late and a little lacking in specifics. It was late because the closer a person gets to being punished for his or her sins, the less impressive the tears. It was lacking in specifics because of his vague confession to "an improper relationship." What would have sounded a lot more sincere would have been to declare, "I have committed adultery. I have lied. I have hated Kenneth Starr. I have sought to destroy the reputations of my critics. I have inflicted a great financial burden upon my staff and friends who have had to hire legal counsel because of my prolonged deceit."

Clinton has evidenced real sorrow in this matter, but

what kind of sorrow? In Paul's second letter to the Corinthians, he writes that, "For godly sorrow worketh repentance to salvation not to be repented of: but the sorrow of the world worketh death" (II Corinthians 7:10). The sorrow that arises from getting caught leads to nothing but death. Godly sorrow leads to repentance—to a different life. Following Clinton's confession at the prayer breakfast, Democratic Senator Bob Kerry of Nebraska said it is inconsistent for the President to confess to the very sins he sends his lawyers out to deny, "The President's lawyers and the President are now saying two different things."

No one knows Clinton's heart but God. Time will reveal whether his repentance is real. Devotional writer Oswald Chambers wrote in *My Utmost for His Highest* that a truly repentant person "proves he is forgiven by being the opposite to what he was, by God's grace. Repentance always brings a man to this point: I have sinned. The surest sign that God is at work is when a man says that and means it."

Cal Thomas says, "the passage of some time is necessary to judge the sincerity of a man for whom truth has not been a strong suit. After his impressive televised performance, Jimmy Swaggart returned to the arms of prostitutes. In spite of Richard Nixon's White House church services....The tape recordings of Oval Office conversations revealed that Mr. Nixon was more gifted in the language of the devil than he was at utterances pleasing to the Lord."[47]

OLD TESTAMENT SCRIPTURES
DEMAND WE TURN FROM OUR SINS

It is impossible to have even an elementary understanding of the Old Testament without understanding that God requires people to repent—to turn from their sins.

Jewish rabbis describe nine activities related to repentance: "Wash you, make you clean; put away the evil of your doings from before mine eyes; cease to do evil; learn to do well; seek judgment, relieve the oppressed, judge the fatherless, plead for the widow. Come now, and let us reason together, saith the LORD: though your sins be as scarlet, they shall be as white as snow; though they be red like crimson, they shall be as wool" (Isaiah 1:16-18). Note carefully the progression: beginning internally with a cleansing, repentance then manifests itself in attitudes and actions. Finally, it results in God's forgiveness.

Isaiah 55:6-7 details the importance of repentance in the Old Testament presentation of salvation: "Seek the Lord while He may be found; call upon Him while He is near. Let the wicked forsake his way and the unrighteous man his thoughts; and let him return to the Lord, and He will have compassion on him, for He will abundantly pardon."

The Jewish prophet Jeremiah lamented, "No man repented him of his wickedness, saying, What have I done? every one turned to his course, as the horse rusheth into the battle" (Jeremiah 8:6). This resulted in God asking a piercing question: "Behold, ye trust in lying words, that cannot profit. Will ye steal, murder, and commit adultery, and swear falsely, and burn incense unto Baal, and walk after other gods whom ye know not; And come and stand before me in this house, which is called by my name, and say, We are delivered to do all these abominations" (Jeremiah 7:8-10).

Ezekiel 18:30 explains that repentance is the way to prevent sin from bringing a life to "ruin": "Therefore I will judge you, O house of Israel, every one according to his ways, saith the Lord GOD. Repent, and turn yourselves from all your transgressions; so iniquity shall not be your ruin."

And Ezekiel 33:18-19 says, 'When the righteous turneth from his righteousness, and committeth iniquity, he shall even die thereby. But if the wicked turn from his wickedness, and do that which is lawful and right, he shall live thereby."

The wicked men of Nineveh saved their city from destruction by giving up their sins: "And God saw their works, that they turned from their evil way; and God repented of the evil, that he had said that he would do unto them; and he did it not" (Jonah 3:10).

THE NEW TESTAMENT DEMANDS
WE TURN FROM OUR SINS

Repentance is not just the teaching of "the old Bible." The New Testament also demands repentance of sins. John the Baptist prepared the way for the coming of Jesus Christ by commanding men to repent: "In those days came John the Baptist, preaching in the wilderness of Judaea, And saying, Repent ye: for the kingdom of heaven is at hand" (Matthew 3:1,2). John demanded more than a shallow profession of repentance, or a religious pedigree. He wanted to see evidence of repentance from sin: "Then said he to the multitude that came forth to be baptized of him, O generation of vipers, who hath warned you to flee from the wrath to come? Bring forth therefore fruits worthy of repentance, and begin not to say within yourselves, We have Abraham to our father: for I say unto you, That God is able of these stones to raise up children unto Abraham" (Luke 3:7,8).

From the early dawn of Christ's ministry, He preached repentance: "From that time Jesus began to preach, and to say, Repent: for the kingdom of heaven is at hand" (Matthew 4:17).

In Matthew 21:32, Jesus taught that people must repent before it becomes possible for them to believe: "For John came unto you in the way of righteousness, and ye believed him not: but the publicans and the harlots believed him: and ye, when ye had seen it, repented not afterward, that ye might believe him."

Jesus explained that He came to earth to persuade people to repent of their sins: "I came not to call the righteous, but sinners to repentance" (Luke 5:32).

When Peter preached on the great day of Pentecost, he commanded, "Repent, and be baptized everyone of you in the name of Jesus Christ for the forgiveness of your sins" (Acts 2:38).

Mark 1:15 says that God requires men to both believe and repent, "And saying, The time is fulfilled, and the kingdom of God is at hand: repent ye, and believe the gospel."

Christ condemned the cities which refused to learn from history that they must repent: "Then began he to upbraid the cities wherein most of his mighty works were done, because they repented not: Woe unto thee, Chorazin! woe unto thee, Bethsaida! for if the mighty works, which were done in you, had been done in Tyre and Sidon, they would have repented long ago in sackcloth and ashes....The men of Nineveh shall rise in judgment with this generation, and shall condemn it: because they repented at the preaching of Jonas; and, behold, a greater than Jonas is here" (Matthew 11:20,21, 12:41).

The disciples of Jesus Christ also spread the message that people must repent: Mark 6:12 says the disciples, "went out, and preached that men should repent."

Luke 15:7 reveals repentance on earth produces happiness in heaven: "I say unto you, that likewise joy shall be in heaven over one sinner that repenteth, more than over ninety and nine just persons, which need no repentance."

Jesus said in Luke 16:30 that a man in hell pleaded for someone to tell his brothers on earth to repent: "And he said, Nay, father Abraham: but if one went unto them from the dead, they will repent."

Christ commissioned the church to preach repentance to the world: "And He said unto them...that repentance and remission of sins should be preached in his name among all nations, beginning at Jerusalem" (Luke 24:44,47).

Acts 2:38 says to receive God's Spirit we must repent: "Then Peter said unto them, Repent, and be baptized every one of you in the name of Jesus Christ for the remission of sins, and ye shall receive the gift of the Holy Ghost."

People must repent before they can be converted and have their sins blotted out. Acts 3:19 says: "Repent ye therefore, and be converted, that your sins may be blotted out, when the times of refreshing shall come from the presence of the Lord."

Jesus was exalted to be a Savior that He might grant repentance: "Him hath God exalted with his right hand to be a Prince and a Saviour, for to give repentance to Israel, and forgiveness of sins" (Acts 5:31).

Acts 8:22 says repentance must precede forgiveness: "Repent therefore of this thy wickedness, and pray God, if perhaps the thought of thine heart may be forgiven thee."

Acts 17:30 says God commands all men to repent: "And the times of this ignorance God winked at; but now commandeth all men every where to repent:"

Christianity's great apostle, Paul, did not hedge on preaching repentance. He said, "I kept back nothing that was profitable unto you, but have showed you, and taught you publicly, and from house to house. Testifying both to the Jews, and also to the Greeks, repentance toward God, and faith toward our Lord Jesus Christ" (Acts 20:21). Note the two things: repentance and faith.

Acts 26:20 tells us the apostle Paul's message was one of repentance—a repentance that proved itself in deeds: "But shewed first unto them of Damascus, and at Jerusalem, and throughout all the coasts of Judaea, and then to the Gentiles, that they should repent and turn to God, and do works meet for repentance."

Paul reminded people in Romans 2:4 that the purpose of God's goodness is to lead them to repentance: "Or despisest thou the riches of his goodness and forbearance and longsuffering; not knowing that the goodness of God leadeth thee to repentance?"

The Bible says Paul rejoiced when men become remorseful enough to repent: "Now I rejoice, not that ye were made sorry, but that ye sorrowed to repentance: for ye were made sorry after a godly manner" (2 Corinthians 7:9).

Paul was heartbroken over church members who had not repented of their sexual immorality: "When I come again, my God will humble me among you, and that I shall bewail many which have sinned already, and have not repented of the uncleanness and fornication and lasciviousness which they have committed" (II Corinthians 12:21).

In II Timothy 2:25, Paul said the purpose of his teaching was to produce repentance, "In meekness instructing those that oppose themselves; if God peradventure will give them repentance to the acknowledging of the truth."

God's great passion is that men might come to repentance: "The Lord is not slack concerning his promise, as some men count slackness; but is longsuffering to us-ward, not willing that any should perish, but that all should come to repentance" (2 Peter 3:9).

Revelation 2:5 warns the church about neglecting repentance: "Remember therefore from whence thou art fallen, and repent, and do the first works; or else I will come unto thee quickly, and will remove thy candlestick out of his place, except thou repent." Nothing is clearer in the New Testament than the necessity of repentance.

JESUS CHRIST DEMANDED
THAT PEOPLE REPENT

When a rich young ruler asked Jesus, "Good master, what good thing shall I do, that I may have eternal life?" Jesus first confronted him with the fact that he was not good. "There is none good but one, that is, God." The rich young ruler asked Jesus which of the Ten Commandments he should keep. Then Jesus held up the second half of the Ten Commandments as a mirror to show him his sinfulness: "Thou shalt do no murder, Thou shalt not commit adultery, Thou shalt not steal, Thou shalt not bear false witness, Honour thy father and thy mother: and, thou shalt love thy neighbour as thyself" The young man, still refusing to recognize his sinfulness and his need for repentance, asked, "All these things have I kept from my youth up: what lack I yet?" Then Jesus drove His point home in a way the young man could not miss. He called on him to repent of his covetousness: "Go and sell that thou hast, and give to the poor, and thou shalt have treasure in heaven: and come and follow me." But, the young man was not willing to repent. "When the young man heard that saying, he went away sorrowful: for he had great possessions" (Matthew 19:16-22). Note the young man had faith that Jesus was a "good Master." But he was not willing to repent of his sin—his money-loving covetousness.

Another wealthy man named Zacchaeus presents an interesting contrast to this young ruler. His first words to Christ were, "Behold, Lord, the half of my goods I give to the poor; and if I have taken any thing from any man by false accusation, I restore him fourfold" (Luke 19:8). Jesus immediately said to him, "Today salvation has come to this house .... For the son of man has come to seek and to save that which was lost" (Luke 19:9-10). Zacchaeus was willing to repent of covetousness and was saved. The rich young ruler refused to repent of his covetousness and went away lost. Had Jesus Christ left out the requirement of repentance, both Zaccheus and the wealthy young ruler would have joined up. He didn't. Jesus didn't exempt those who are rulers from having to repent.

THE CHURCH'S HISTORIC TRADITION
OF DEMANDING REPENTANCE

The incident that symbolically marked the beginning of the Reformation was Martin Luther's posting of his *Ninety-five Theses* on the door of the Wittenberg Castle Church in 1517. The first four of the theses show clearly what Luther thought of the necessity of repentance:

"1. Our Lord and Master Jesus Christ, in saying, 'Repent ye,' etc., meant the whole life of the faithful to be an act of repentance.

2. This saying cannot be understood of the sacrament of penance (i.e. of confession and absolution) which is administered by the priesthood.

3. Yet he does not mean interior repentance only; nay, interior repentance is void if it does not produce different kinds of mortifications of the flesh.

4. And so penance remains while self-hate remains (i.e. true interior repentance); namely right up to entrance into the kingdom of heaven."

The catechism of the Presbyterian church, which was founded by John Knox, says: "Repentance unto life is a saving grace whereby a sinner, out of a true sense of his sin and apprehension of the mercy of God in Christ, doth with grief and hatred of his sin turn from it unto God with full purpose of an endeavor after new obedience."

Charles Haddon Spurgeon, perhaps the most famous pastor of the 20th century wrote: "Another proof of the conquest of a soul for Christ will be found in *a real change of life*. If the man does not live differently from what he did before, both at home and abroad, his repentance needs to be repented of, and his conversion is a fiction. Not only action and language, but spirit and temper must be changed. Abiding under the power of any known sin is a mark of our being the servants of sin, for 'his servants ye are to whom ye obey.' Idle are the boasts of a man who harbors within himself the love of any transgression. He may feel what he likes, and believe what he likes, he is still in the gall of bitterness and the bonds of iniquity while a single sin rules his heart and life. True regeneration implants a hatred of all evil; and where one sin is delighted in, the evidence is fatal to a sound hope .... There must be a harmony between the life and the profession. A Christian professes to renounce sin; and if he does not do so, his very name is an imposture."[48]

Billy Sunday, the evangelist who held the largest meeting in American history, with over 2 million attending his New York City crusade, demanded that people quit their whiskey drinking and adultery. Tens of thousand did and the leaders of the liquor industry were alleged to have wanted to kill him. It took an army of police to get him in and out of his crusades.

IT IS PROFITABLE FOR PREACHERS
TO IGNORE PREACHING REPENTANCE

Why have preachers failed to tell Clinton he must turn from his sins? Scripture suggests such preachers are hucksters, men who profit off of a phony gospel. In II Corinthians 2:17, Paul says, "For we are not as many, which corrupt the word of God." Missionary James Stewart, in his book *Evangelism*, explains, "The word *corrupt* is a very interesting word. It is an old Anglo-Saxon word meaning a huckster. A huckster was a retailer of articles like a peddler or hawker, in contrast to a merchant. The word also refers to a seller of wine. Some wine sellers diluted the drink for commercial gain and thereby became 'hucksters.' See Isaiah 1:22 which says, 'Wine sellers mix the wine with water.' The huckster adulterated his goods for the purpose of catering to the tastes of the people, to beat competitors, or for sordid gain. Even in Paul's day there were hucksters of the Word of God. Their aim was to make their wares acceptable."[49]

"In America, more than anywhere else, there is a tendency to employ the methods of modern business, high-pressure advertising, public opinion polls, mass suggestion, and success stories to swing the masses into the church," states James Stewart, in his book, *Evangelism*. "The danger of this technique lies in the subtle shift of emphasis from the objective truth of the Christian Gospel to its pragmatic value to society. The result . . . is to transform the Gospel challenge of 'repent and believe' into the cynical technique of *How to Win Friends and Influence People.*"[50]

FOUR WAYS CLERGYMEN TRY
TO GET AROUND REPENTANCE

How have Clinton's Clergymen excused their blatant disregard for repentance? How can highly respected ministers justify courting the favor of a powerful political figure rather than the favor of heaven's most-high God? How do preachers live with themselves when they disobey Christ's command and deny His example regarding repentance? Perhaps the comedian W. C. Fields gave us an insight. When asked if he was reading the Bible because he had become religious, he replied,

"No. I am looking for loopholes." Preachers like Clinton's Clergymen typically try to crawl through four loopholes to get out of preaching repentance.

1. "Side Stepping Grace"

First, they say if man has to repent, then salvation is by works, man saves himself by his own efforts and has no need for the grace of God. Paul countered this by declaring repentance was not a mere human work but a gift to those who wanted it: "If God peradventure will give them repentance to the acknowledging of the truth: and that they may recover themselves out of the snare of the devil, who are taken captive by him at his will" (II Timothy 2:25-26). The news of sinners repenting caused the early church to glorify God. They did not see repentance as the mere work of man: "When they heard these things, they held their peace, and glorified God, saying, Then hath God also to the Gentiles granted repentance unto life" (Acts 11:18). Repentance is not simply a human work. It involves a man being "willing" to turn from his sins and God then empowering him to overcome the passions of his sin.

2. "Repentance is an Outdated Doctrine"

Second, some who would pervert the teaching of repentance say it was only required in another age; repentance is not required today. Dr. Ironsides, though a firm dispensationalist (one who separates the different ways and times God has of dealing with mankind), denounced such ideas: "Our Lord's solemn words, 'Except ye repent, ye shall all likewise perish,' are as important today as when first uttered....No dispensational distinctions, important as these are in understanding and interpreting God's ways with man, can alter this truth."[51]

3. "All we Need is Faith"

Third, those who deny the need for repentance insist faith alone is sufficient. Yet Paul makes it clear that believing and repenting are the two inseparable sides of genuine faith: "In every place your faith to God-ward is spread abroad...ye turned to God from idols to serve the living and true God" (I Thessalonians 1:8,9).

4. "Grace is Sufficient"

Fourth, the enemies of repentance say we are saved by grace alone. That is correct. But before God gives the gift of salvation, He first gives the gift of repentance and of faith to the willing soul. The Bible clearly teaches that "The grace of God that bringeth salvation hath appeared to all men, Teaching us that, denying ungodliness and worldly lusts, we should live soberly, righteously, and godly, in this present world" (Titus 2:11,12). The free gift of grace includes more than forgiveness and a home in heaven. It also includes the desire and the power to turn from our sins and live a righteous life. This is all in the gift package. So, if grace has not taught a person to live soberly and righteously in this world, it is not the grace that will bring salvation in the next world.

Trying to climb through these loopholes, Clinton's clergymen have failed him. The President does not bear all the responsibility for his fall. His guilt lies in not repenting of his sins, and his clergymen must bear the responsibility for not telling him that God demands repentance of sin. Had the Clinton Clergy been faithful to their call—had they delivered the true message of the Bible during Clinton's early years, it could have made a big difference. At best, Bill Clinton might have repented of the adultery, lying and selfish abuse of power that have disgraced him. At worst, the minister's hands would be clean from the blood of a fallen President.

Chapter Four

EVERYBODY LIES

Rev. Jesse Jackson was drilled on TV about President Clinton's lying: "What about the seven months of false denials? How did he feel when he learned the truth?" Jackson replied, "Let me tell you about sin and shame and lies." Then he retraced the story of Genesis, of Adam and Eve sinning by eating the forbidden fruit: "They react with shame, trying to cover up their bodies. Then they lie about what they did and why. 'Why do you lie? Because you're afraid. That's part of the human condition,' Jackson says. 'What is the solution?' Atonement, repentance, forgiveness, redemption.'' [52] With this smooth Biblical presentation, Jackson paints lying as just a natural part of the "human condition," like eating, sleeping and breathing. It is understandable why Rev. Jackson goes easy on those who dodge the truth. Jackson can say he is for abortion and against abortion without blinking an eye. This declared abortion supporter has written:

"There are those who argue that the right to privacy is of [a] higher order than the right to life ... that was the premise of slavery. You could not protest the existence or treatment of slaves on the plantation because that was private and therefore outside your right to be concerned. What happens to the mind of a person, and the moral fabric of a nation, that accepts the aborting of the life of a baby without a pang of conscience? What kind of a person and what kind of a society will we have 20 years hence if life can be taken so casually? It is that question, the question of our attitude, our value system, and our mind-set with regard to the nature and worth of life itself that is the central question confronting mankind. Failure to answer that question affirmatively may leave us with a hell right here on earth."

Rev. Jackson wrote the above statements in a 1977 National Right to Life News article. He also endorsed the Hyde Amendment in an open letter to Congress that opposed federal funds used for "killing infants."

LEGACY OF LIES

By downplaying the Bible's teaching on lying, Clinton's clergymen have produced a deceptive disciple. Washington Post columnist Richard Cohen in his December 22, 1998 column, said, "He is a sneaky guy, dripping charm and lies like a headwaiter promising a table in a few minutes. He bested the GOP repeatedly, sometimes by dealing from the bottom of the deck. He lied to Gingrich and to other congressional leaders, causing them to sputter with fury." Cohen, who supports Clinton, said, "He was smarter than they were and traveled lighter, unburdened by matters of conscience. To Clinton, lies and truth are equally useful. If one won't do, try the other."

Stanley A. Renshon, a professor of Political Science at the City University of New York and a certified psychoanalyst, says Clinton "is a mother's dream and most fathers' nightmare, (a) decidedly charming suitor, but with a moral compass frozen at self-interest....he remains a man of puzzling and inconsistent political principles—announcing that 'the era of big government is over' even as he unveils dozens of new initiatives.'"[53]

In 1993, when asked about eating fast food, Clinton replied, "I don't eat much junk food." He later amended his remark by explaining, "I don't necessarily consider McDonald's junk food. I eat at McDonald's and Burger King and these other fast-food places. A lot of them have very nutritious food...chicken sandwiches...salads..."

Clinton has bragged about his low golf scores, but one reporter said he saw him take three tee-shots on one hole (only one is legal). *The St. Petersburg Times*, referring to the lie about Lewinsky, reported, "President Clinton, who habitually has lied about everything from marijuana to his golf score, has been caught in his biggest and broadest lie yet."[54]

In 1996, President Clinton said he has "vivid and painful" childhood memories of black-church burnings in Arkansas. The director of the Arkansas History Commission corrected the President by saying, "I've never known of a black church being burned in Arkansas."[55]

In 1990, gubernatorial candidate Clinton was asked, "Will you guarantee to us that, if re-elected, there is absolutely, positively no way that you'll run for any other political office and that you'll serve out your term in full?" Clinton replied, "You bet...That's the job I want. That's the job I'll do for the next four years." The following year, Clinton announced his candidacy for president. Of course, Clinton didn't lie. He just deceived by not even answering the question. He just said, "you bet" but if you had bet on it you would have lost.

During Clinton's 1992 presidential campaign, he said that "it was simply a fluke that I wasn't called" to serve in the Vietnam War. "I was just lucky, I guess," he declared. Clinton expanded his remarks, saying that he "never received any unusual or favorable treatment" that helped him avoid the draft. In truth, Clinton received an induction notice while at Oxford in 1969 and asked the draft board to postpone it until the end of the term, after which he enrolled in an ROTC program in Arkansas. A well-connected uncle successfully lobbied the board on Clinton's behalf.

"I am opposed to abortion and to government funding of abortions. We should not spend state funds on abortions because so many people believe abortion is wrong," Clinton said in a letter to Arkansas Right to Life, September 26, 1986. Yet, he fought every pro-life effort.

After promising the "most ethical administration" in history, Clinton has "presided over one in which resignations for ethical cause, indictments, convictions, judicial repri-mands, appointments of special investigative prosecutors, and continuing questions about ethical and possibly criminal be-havior have played a defining role," say Stanley Renshon.[56]

Clinton denied having a 12-year affair with Gennifer Flowers. Of course, that would not be a lie if he in fact had a 13-year affair with her. Later, he admitted that he had sex one time with the attractive lounge singer. I feel sure that he thought he was being truthful, since he did not say he *only* had sex with her once.

Stanley A. Renshon asks, "What can we say of a president who looks the public directly in the eye, enlists his wife to bolster his deceit, and then flatly denies what he has now confessed to in the semi-privacy of sealed court testi-mony: that Gennifer Flowers was telling the truth, and he wasn't."[57]

Beginning in 1987, he repeatedly told reporters inquiring about his past drug use that he had "never broken the laws of my state" or "country." But in 1992 when pressed about whether he had broken any state, national or international laws, Clinton admitted, "I've never broken a state law, but when I was in England I experimented with marijuana a time or two, and I didn't like it. I didn't inhale and never tried it again."

In the President's 1996 State of the Union Address, he declared that "the era of big government is over." Yet that address contained a large list of new government initiatives that required expanding government.

Clinton's friends defend him with these talking points: (1) even if Clinton is lying, it has to do with sex; (2) even if Clinton is lying, the vast right-wing conspiracy is out to get him; (3) even if Clinton is lying, Starr is a really, deeply evil man; (4) even if Clinton is lying, his poll numbers are high; and so on. Note that no one denies that he is lying (except political commentator Eleanor Clift and the First Lady, who go beyond the call of duty to earn their presidential kneepads).

Clinton promised during the 1992 campaign that "[If] I catch anybody [going through State Department personnel files] I will fire them the next day. You won't have to have an inquiry or rigamarde or anything else.'"[58] But when a longtime Democratic Party political operative ended up with sensitive FBI files on Republican leaders, Clinton explained that it was just a "bureaucratic error."

On June 21, 1998 the Justice Department announced that handgun background checks mandated by the Brady law resulted in 69,000 people being denied permission to purchase guns in 1997. On the same day, the White House issued a statement that said President Clinton proclaimed that, "law enforcement officials have stopped hundreds of thousands of felons, fugitives and stalkers from buying handguns every year."[59]

On Saturday, January 17, 1998 President Clinton became the first President to give a deposition in his own case.[60] He had "difficulty" remembering many things Paula Jones lawyers asked about, like the gifts Monica Lewinsky had given him. But Clinton was able to recall his moralistic opposition to the consumption of alcoholic beverages clearly:

Q: What did you have to drink?
A: I don't remember.
Q: Was it alcoholic?
A: Oh, no, no, I don't serve alcohol there in the office of the White House.
Q: Not ever?
A: Never.

When asked about his relations with Miss Lewinsky, Clinton was emphatic.
Q: Did you have an extramarital sexual affair with Monica Lewinsky?
A: No.
Q: If she told someone that she had a sexual affair with you beginning in November of 1995, would that be a lie?
A: It's certainly not the truth. It would not be the truth.
Q: I think I used the term "sexual affair." And so the record is completely clear, have you ever had sexual relations with Monica Lewinsky, as that term is defined in Deposition Exhibit 1, as modified by the Court?
A: I have never had sexual relations with Monica Lewinsky. I've never had an affair with her.
Later Mr. Clinton would admit: "When I was alone with Ms. Lewinsky on certain occasions... I engaged in conduct that was

wrong." DNA evidence proved he had.

When the President was asked, during the Paula Jones deposition, "at any time have you and Monica Lewinsky ever been alone together in any room in the White House?" the President answered, "I have no specific recollection." Yet, in Monica Lewinsky's grand jury testimony, she testified that they had engaged in a sexual encounter just 20 days previous to Clinton's statement.

In response to the question, "Have you ever given gifts to Monica Lewinsky?" Mr. Clinton said, "I don't recall." Yet, the record shows that two and a half weeks earlier he had given her six gifts.

When asked if he had ever talked with Monica Lewinsky about the possibility of her testifying in the Jones lawsuit, Mr. Clinton answered, "I'm not sure." Yet, we know that Lewinsky says she spoke to him about her testimony on December 17, 1997 (by phone), December 28, 1997 (in person) and January 5, 1998 (by phone).

President Clinton testified under oath 100 times that he could not remember details about his relationship with Monica Lewinsky. Yet, one of his closest associates, Vernon Jordan, says Clinton has "an extraordinary memory, one of the greatest memories" he has ever seen in a political figure.

On January 26, the day before his State of the Union address, the president went before the cameras in the Roosevelt Room of the White House, with his wife at his side. There he told the lie that will resonate through history: "I want to say one thing to the American people. I want you to listen to me. I'm going to say this again. I did not have sexual relations with that woman—Miss Lewinsky." Later the President would be forced to admit he had misled the American people and had engaged in an "inappropriate relationship" with Miss Lewinsky.

WITNESSES TESTIFY TO
PRESIDENT CLINTON'S DECEPTION

Charles Krauthammer made this observation about this telling moment of the Clinton presidency: "He takes to TV and delivers one of the most skillfully faked bald-faced lies in American history, a lie delivered, in the words of his loyal friend of 30 years, Robert Reich, with 'passionate intensity' and 'stunning conviction' recalling 'the great Method actors of a previous generation.' Result? His polls soar."[61]

Dee Dee Myers, President Clinton's press secretary in 1993 and 1994, expressed shock at the number of visits Lewinsky made to the White House. She said she herself had not visited the White House that many times since leaving. "There's no way to convince the American people that thirty-seven visits to the White House by a former intern is routine. That's extraordinary... and raises a lot of questions." After Clinton confessed to misleading the public, Myers expressed her hurt over his lies. In an article titled "That's Where He Lost Me," she says, "Since January, I've been asked often if I was surprised by allegations that the President had an affair with a 21-year-old intern. I wasn't. After all, as the Clintons are quick to point out, they've been accused of everything from adultery to drug running to murder. What surprised me in this case was this: it was true....I learned to be careful with Clinton's words, for he chose them carefully....When he said the Gennifer Flowers story wasn't true, for example, he meant it. But he didn't mean that part of it might not be true....He knew the consequences of getting caught, but he went ahead. For 18 months. In the West Wing of the White House. When he was caught, he put all

his chips on the same kind of artfully worded, misleading denials that had snatched him from the brink of
disaster before. And for seven months he put his
family, his friends, his staff and his supporters through
hell....It would be easier if I didn't like him, and
cherish memories of political achievements and personal moments. It would be easier if I didn't believe in
his agenda or think he was a potentially great President. But I do. I just wish he had done right by all the
people who so willingly gave him their votes, their
hopes, their labor and their love."[62]

Stephen L. Carter, a professor at Yale and author of
Civility: Manners, Morals and the Etiquette of Democracy,
said, "Everyone now knows that he had an intimate relationship with a 21-year-old White House intern and spent seven
months lying about it to the public, to his family and to
investigators. His Presidency is so hobbled that when United
States armed forces attacked terrorist targets in Afghanistan
and the Sudan...many Americans wondered whether the President just wanted to distract the public from the scandal."

George Stephanopoulos, former senior Clinton aide,
said of the Lewinsky affair: "These are probably the most
serious allegations yet leveled against the president. There's no
question that...if they're true, they're not only politically dam-
aging but it could lead to impeachment proceedings." He
elaborated later, saying Clinton had violated a "loyalty con-
tract" with the American people by asking people to lie: "I
don't think a president is loyal to his people if he either
knowingly asks them to lie or asks them to say things which he
realizes are not very credible, asks them to take him on his
word without giving them reasons to take him at his word.
And I think that is the trap that the president has set right
now."[63]

Mrs. Clinton said on national TV she would be upset if her husband had an affair and lied to cover it. On the *NBC Today Show*, she said, "If all that were proven true, I think that would be a very serious offense." When Mrs. Clinton emerged from the White House on August 14 for a South Lawn birthday party for her husband, her friends whispered that something was wrong. "I thought they'd just had one of their fights in the residence," says a friend. "She was so cold that all of us felt frostbitten. I look back on it and I see one very hurt lady. She barely spoke to us."[64] Few women in history have ever had to endure such a public exposure of private betrayals. Mrs. Clinton felt the full impact of how hurtful lying can be.

Dr. Robert Schuller, the pastor who provided Clinton with the Bible phrase "healer of the breach," from Isaiah 58:12, expressed his disappointment in the President. When Schuller met with the President in the Oval Office, the President vehemently denied a sexual relationship with Monica Lewinsky. "He did it with such passion and with his eyes locked on me," Schuller said. "He lied. Blatantly. He's the third public man to do that to me—Nixon and Agnew lied to me, bluntly, boldly. And now Clinton."[65]

William J. Bennett, former Secretary of Education, said: "Mr. Clinton is a calculating, inveterate, constant liar. He lied to his family, his friends, his lawyers, his aides, his Cabinet, his party and, emphatically, to his fellow citizens. He lied in civil litigation and before a federal grand jury. He lied repeatedly, with forethought and malice, with the intent to corrupt justice. And he is lying to this day."[66]

Andy Rooney, the *60 Minutes* commentator, says, "Watching the videotaped testimony of the president before the remote grand jury reminded me of when *Associated Press* reporter Terry Anderson was imprisoned in Lebanon and forced, by his captors, to sit on a straight chair in an empty room in front of a camera with bright lights shining in his face and lie to the American people. It was like having an animal in your headlights scurrying across the road, trying desperately not to be run over. Clinton got run over."

THE GOVERNMENT TREATS LYING
AS A SERIOUS CRIME

Reporters Bob Woodward and Carl Bernstein said, during the Watergate investigation of Richard Nixon, "The problem is not Watergate or the cover-up....It's that he hasn't been telling the truth to the American people....The tape makes it evident that he hasn't leveled with the country for probably eighteen months. And the President can't lead a country he has deliberately misled for a year and a half."[67] Ann Coulter, in her book *High Crimes and Misdemeanors*, interestingly reveals, "That, incidentally, was how Nixon's speech writer, Pat Buchanan, explained to Julie Nixon that her father had to go."[68]

Proverbs 25:19 says, "Confidence in an unfaithful man in time of trouble is like a broken tooth, and a foot out of joint...." When you put your confidence in a man without character, without honor or integrity, it's like having your foot out of joint and a broken tooth. It hurts. "Integrity without knowledge is weak and useless, and knowledge without integrity is dangerous and dreadful," said Samuel Johnson. The Watergate special prosecutor, Leon Jaworski, said of Nixon's disgrace and resignation: "What sank him was his lying.... People can tolerate a great deal in their public officials. If a person is big enough to say 'I did it,' he'll be forgiven."[69]

Ann Coulter, the legal affairs correspondent for HUMAN EVENTS, says false statements have traditionally led to impeachment, "The only impeachment convictions ever rendered by the United States Senate were for the high crimes and misdemeanors of: Drunkenness and Senility; Incitement to Revolt and Rebellion Against the Nation; Bribery; Kickbacks and Tax Evasion; Tax Evasion; Conspiracy to Solicit a Bribe; and False Statements to a Grand Jury."[70] She points out, "Nixon was forced to resign for acting in a manner 'subversive of constitutional government'...Nixon's subversion consisted of: One presidential lie, one invocation of presidential privilege, and zero criminal offenses."[71]

The government has historically taken lying a lot more seriously than the Clinton Clergy as this impeachment record shows:

- Judge Walter Nixon was impeached on May 10, 1989. His crime was lying about interfering with the criminal prosecution of his business partner's son, who had been accused of drug smuggling. Article One of his impeachment said: "In the course of his grand jury testimony and having taken an oath that he would tell the truth, the whole truth and nothing but the truth, Judge Nixon did knowingly and contrary to his oath make a material false or misleading statement to the grand jury....Wherefore, Judge Walter H. Nixon Jr. is guilty of an impeachable offense and should be removed from office."

- Judge Alcee Hastings, presently a Democratic U. S. Representative from Florida, was impeached in 1988 for making false statements in a case involving bribery and sentence reductions.

- Barbara Battalino, formerly a hospital physician with the Veterans Administration, was fined $3,500 and ordered to serve a year of probation after she admitted giving false testimony in a federal civil proceeding.

- Judge Harry Claiborne did "willfully and knowingly" file a false return with the IRS, a form of lying under oath since he signed a statement swearing the information he provided was true. In July 1986, this judge of the U. S. District Court for the District of Nevada was impeached for his false statements.[72]

- President Richard Nixon was forced to resign from the presidency for one presidential lie and one invocation of presidential privilege.[73] In a document dealing with Nixon's impeachment, dated Aug. 20, 1974, the House of Representatives formally accused Nixon of "(1) making or causing to be made false or misleading statements to lawfully authorized investigative officers and employees of the United States; (2) withholding relevant and material evidence or information from lawfully authorized and investigative officers and employees of the United States; (3) approving, condoning, acquiescing in and counseling witnesses with respect to the giving of false or misleading statements to lawfully authorized investigative officers and employees of the United States and false or misleading testimony in duly instituted judicial and congressional proceedings." One of the lawyers who prepared this statement was Hillary Rodham Clinton.[74]

- The government has not only impeached officials for lying under oath, it has imprisoned ordinary citizens for lying under oath and even when it was about sex. On Tuesday, December 1, 1998 Pam Parsons and Barbara Battalino, both serving time for perjury, testified before the House Judiciary Committee. Parsons, a former women's basketball coach at the University of South Carolina, told about pleading guilty to perjury after she lied in a libel suit regarding a sexual relationship she had with one of her players. Battalinno, a former Veterans' Administration psychiatrist, related how she was fined and placed under house arrest after it was proven she lied about her sexual relation with a former patient. Judiciary Committee member Bill McCollum, R-Fla., said, "These are average citizens who have been found guilty of perjury, prosecuted by the Clinton administration. Is it fair for them to be serving a sentence and the president not be impeached?"[185]

GOD TREATS LYING
AS A SERIOUS SIN

When God gave the Ten Commandments, He declared, "Thou shalt not bear false witness" (Exodus 20:16). God wrote this in a tablet of stone to emphasize just how important honesty is. Stop and think about how many times we stake our lives on men telling the truth. The weatherman tells our pilot there is no storm; if he is lying we might crash. The electrical inspector says our home is up to code; if he is lying we might burn to death. The pharmacist tell us the pills are right; if he is lying we might die. Alexander Pope said, "An honest man is the noblest work of God." And a dishonest man the most tragic.

When is it right to lie? Only when breaking this commandment would prevent breaking a greater command. If a prisoner of war could prevent the death of his squad by lying to his captors, this would be the moral thing to do. Outside of circumstances as unique as this, lying is always wrong.

Jeremiah cried out against the false prophets in Jerusalem who affected the morals of the people: "I have seen in the prophets of Jerusalem an horrible thing: They commit adultery and walk in lies...none doth return from his wickedness: they are all of them unto me as Sodom, and the inhabitants thereof as Gomorrah....For from the prophets of Jerusalem is profaneness gone forth into all of the land" (Jeremiah 23:14,15).

The very first qualification the Bible gives for leaders in the New Testament church was that they be "men of honest report" (Acts 6:3).

When the sin of Israel's King Saul was exposed, the King greatly compounded his problems by lying. "And Samuel came to Saul: and Saul said unto him, Blessed be thou of the LORD: I have performed the commandment of the LORD" (I Samuel 15:13). Then, when the bleating of sheep he was commanded to kill gave him away, he lied again and blamed other people. "And Saul said, They have brought them from the Amalekites: for the people spared the best of the sheep and of the oxen, to sacrifice unto the LORD (vs. 15). Saul's lie cost him his kingdom: "The LORD hath rejected thee from being king over Israel" (vs. 26). King Saul discovered he did not have "executive privilege" when it came to lying.

An anonymous writer said, "When wealth is lost, nothing is lost; When health is lost, something is lost; When character is lost, all is lost." Tracing the consequences of lying in the case of Saul and Clinton, it becomes clear that by lying all is lost. Although those men both lied, there is a marked difference between the two. Saul's preacher Samuel stood face to face with him and condemned his evil. Clinton's clergymen failed to tell their President the truth.

There was a time when Bill Clinton supported God's command against lying. During Nixon's Watergate troubles, Clinton said, "If a President of the United States ever lied to the American people, he should resign."

Chapter Five

IT'S JUST ABOUT SEX

Mrs. Clinton was reported to be very hurt when she heard about the book her husband had given to his girlfriend, Monica Lewinsky. She is said to have been aboard an Amtrak train when she learned her husband had sent Lewinsky the *Leaves of Grass*. She told a friend, "He gave me the same book after our second date!" The book is quite sexual: "You settled your head athwart my hips and gently turn'd over upon me."[75] It must have been a small comfort to Mrs. Clinton to hear Rev. Jesse Jackson and other clergymen say that is was "just about sex."

Rev. Jackson downplayed adultery on CNN by making comparisons with Biblical figures such as Samson. He pointed out that Samson had been tempted by Delilah but God gave him another chance. "Yet the special prosecutor, I suppose, would have locked him up," he observed. Rev. Jackson needs to take time to read that Samson was arrested, and imprisoned, and died a prisoner of his captors. And it was "just sex" with Delilah that brought him down.

Apparently the President and many others find it difficult to understand why anything as "enjoyable" as adultery could be very wrong. Even the Bible recognizes the attraction of the forbidden act. It portrays the adulteress tempting her prey with the words: "Stolen waters are sweet, and bread eaten in secret is pleasant" (Proverbs 9:17). The Bible declares adultery is "sweet" and very "pleasant." It is a titillating experience quite different from anything the secure, committed marriage relationship has to offer. The reason lies in the fact it is "stolen."

Stealing sex, like stealing money can be exciting. There is no comparison between the thrill of robbing a bank and picking up your paycheck at the company office. Any bank robber will say there is no rush like walking into a bank knowing that in 40 seconds the police will come roaring up, with sirens blaring and guns firing. In less than a minute you may be running our of the bank with pockets full of money, or you may be carried out dead. Likewise, to steal the forbidden kisses of one who is not your mate excites. There is a rush. But the price for adultery, like that of bankrobbing, can run extremely high. Bill Clinton is just beginning to learn how high.

PREACHING AGAINST A RULER'S SEXUAL INDULGENCES CAN BE COSTLY

History offers stern lessons for those who preach against a ruler's adultery. Sir Thomas More, "the man for all seasons," refused to approve a divorce for Henry VIII from Catherine of Aragon and to acknowledge Henry as the supreme head of the Church of England. More was a man who stood staunchly on the sexual principles of the Bible. For this he was executed. Then Henry VIII, having silenced the voice of God's messenger, freely indulged himself in sexual pleasures. After marrying six women, he died from a venereal disease. Even though it was "just about sex," More took an unbending stand against Henry VIII—a stand that cost him his life.

John the Baptist got into serious trouble when he told King Herod it was not lawful for him to sleep with his brother's wife: "Herod had laid hold on John, and bound him, and put him in prison for Herodias' sake, his brother Philip's wife. For John said unto him, It is not lawful for thee to have her....And he sent, and beheaded John in the prison" (Matthew 14:3,4,10). Even though it was "just about sex," John the Baptist was more concerned about the soul of Herod than he was about his own life. His commitment was to his Lord, not to self-preservation.

Kenneth Starr, an active Christian who exposed Clinton's adultery, has suffered from the sword of character assassination and mockery. Clinton associate James Carville ridiculed Starr for singing hymns as he walks along the Potomac River: "That's all that man's about....It's about sex....He plants a story, he goes down by the Potomac and listens to hymns, as the cleansing waters of the Potomac go by, and we are going to wash all the Sodomites and fornicators out of town."[76]

Historically, Christians like Sir Thomas More and John the Baptist who do not keep quiet about a ruler's sexual dalliances pays a terrible price. Clinton's clergymen have not been willing to pay that price.

Had one of the Clinton's Clergy strongly rebuked him for his sexual conduct, that minister might have lost access to the President. He might have been investigated by the IRS. He could have had an FBI check into his past. On the other hand, he might have won the soul of Clinton and prevented the whole tragedy. The minister would have certainly preserved his integrity.

REV. JACKSON COMFORTED CLINTON
WHEN HIS ADULTERY WAS EXPOSED

Instead of offering a strong rebuke, Rev. Jesse Jackson defended Bill Clinton's adultery by saying his actions are just something men "naturally do." In other words, God made our bodies and our bodies just naturally desire to commit adultery. Therefore, if anyone is to be blamed for adultery, it must be God! Jackson's reasoning sounds like the cannibal who said if God had not meant for us to eat people, he wouldn't have made them taste so good.

The Rev. Jackson's idea that adultery is just a natural thing that men do is refuted by scientific data. A survey from the National Opinion Research Center at the University of Chicago shows 21 percent of men and 11 percent of women have committed adultery at some point in their married lives. The numbers are only 3.6 percent of men and 1.3 percent of women who report to have committed adultery in the past twelve months.[77] The figures indicate that men "just naturally" refrain from adultery, rather than commit it, as Jackson said. So if an individual moves in a circle where "everyone" habitually commits adultery, that person's circle of friends is an unusually immoral group of people.

When Rev. Jackson was preparing for his second presidential bid, rumors of extramarital affairs circulated. His wife took the position that she did not want to know about the matter. ``I don't believe in examining sheets. That's a violation of privacy,'' Jacqueline Jackson told a *Life* reporter in June 1987. ``If my husband has committed adultery, he better not tell me. And you better not go digging into it because I'm trying to raise a family and won't let you be the one to destroy my family," she said.[78]

Rev. Jackson has been in regular contact with the Clintons during the Monica Lewinsky scandal. Jackson told reporters he did not request, and the President did not give, detailed information about the scandal. "We never got into the preciseness of the situation because as a minister and as an adult who is not naive, I did not need the lurid details to look at the range of possibilities and consequences," Jackson explained.[79] How could he consider the consequence of eternal damnation for adultery and the consequence of eternal life for those delivered out of it and not cry for the President's deliverance from the sin? It is surprising that a man bearing the title of "Reverend" has declared how natural, rather than how wicked, adultery is.

WASHINGTON PASTOR DECLARES FAITHFULNESS TO YOUR MATE JUST A MATTER OF "CULTURAL PREFERENCE"

Rev. J. Philip Wogaman, the pastor of the church Bill and Hillary Clinton attend in Washington, told the *New York Times* that when people make a "cultural expression" like heterosexuality or marital fidelity into a moral absolute, they have fallen into "idolatry." William J. Bennett responded by saying: "His casual dismissal of sexual fidelity as merely a "cultural expression" is hubris of a high order; he is dismissing the accumulated wisdom of the centuries and the clear teaching of his professed faith. He is also making the widespread (postmodern) philosophical error of assuming that morality is merely a product of culture, and that there is no such thing as objective truth. As for moral absolutes turning into "idolatry": Christ taught that the mark of a true believer was to 'keep My commandment' of which sexual fidelity is one."[80]

Wogaman says choosing to be faithful to your mate is a cultural expression similar to putting ice in your soda in America and leaving it out in Europe. Choosing heterosexuality instead of homosexuality is like men wearing kilts in Scotland and pants in America. Just cultural preferences!

Some thought Evangelist Billy Graham minimized Clinton's guilt when he told *The Today Show* viewers on March 5, 1998, that he forgives President Bill Clinton because "I know the frailty of human nature . . . He has such a tremendous personality that I think the ladies just go wild over him." Graham also explained Mr. Clinton's sexual weakness by stating, "We're living in a whole different world today, and the pressure on anybody today is difficult."

In his editorial "Billy Graham Should Remember the White House is Not in Heaven," Cal Thomas responded to Graham's forgiveness of Clinton prior to the President admitting he had sinned: "In offering Clinton 'forgiveness,' Graham is suggesting there is something to forgive. Clinton has stated publicly he 'never had a sexual relationship with that woman, Ms. Lewinsky.' So for what exactly is Graham forgiving the president? At what point would Graham point his finger and, like the prophet Nathan, say, 'Thou art the man'?"

"Billy Graham is a kind, non-controversial man who is by nature gracious to other people," wrote Thomas. "While I am sure that this beloved minister meant to show the most outstanding virtue of forgiveness, his words left much room for people to misunderstand him. He said the President is a 'strong, vigorous young man' who has a 'tremendous personality,' and 'the ladies just go wild' over him (indicating that the women, not the president, are the aggressors in his sexual escapades). Adultery was minimized."

Thomas, who has known Billy Graham for nearly 30 years and has written in glowing terms of the evangelist's supreme integrity, suggests, "Now that he is in the twilight of his life, at age 79, and suffering from Parkinson's disease, perhaps he and all preachers should impose a moratorium on schmoozing with presidents and focus solely on building the Kingdom of God, which is not of this world."[81]

THE DAVID DOCTRINE
OF SEXUAL MORALITY

Rev. Wogaman rushed to Clinton's defense when his adultery became public: "King David did something that was much worse than anything that President Clinton is alleged to have done. And King David, if I read my Bible correctly, was not impeached."[82] On the Sunday prior to his testimony before the grand jury, Clinton aides told reporters that the President had been reading Psalm 51, a passage that begins, "Have mercy upon me, O God . . . blot out my transgressions." And one memorable punctuation in his statement Monday night was, "This is between me, the two people I love the most . . . and our God."[83] This passage—Psalm 51—has been fashioned into "The David Doctrine of Sexual Morality." After Clinton's fall, his clergymen have attempted to shield him by drawing comparisons between his sins and those of King David. The doctrine goes like this: David saw another man's wife, Bathsheba, took her, and committed adultery with her. Since the Bible says David was allowed to continue as king, adultery couldn't be too bad. Therefore, if we would be like God, we must allow an adulterous Clinton to continue as President. Besides, David prayed "Restore unto me the joy of thy salvation." This means he did not lose his salvation for committing adultery, he only lost the joy of that salvation.

Here is what Clinton's Clergymen have failed to mention:

(1) There was no legal process for impeaching kings in Israel. His son Absolem tried to have him removed from office. He and his followers were killed.

(2) As far as David being allowed to continue as the king, God never wanted Israel to have a king. It was done at the people's insistence and looked upon by God as a punishment upon them. Here is the Bible's account of how David's position was created:

> "Make us a king to judge us like all the nations. But the thing displeased Samuel, when they said, Give us a king to judge us. And Samuel prayed unto the LORD. And the LORD said unto Samuel, Hearken unto the voice of the people in all that they say unto thee: for they have not rejected thee, but they have rejected me, that I should not reign over them....Now therefore hearken unto their voice: howbeit yet protest solemnly unto them, and shew them the manner of the king that shall reign over them.

> "And Samuel told all the words of the LORD unto the people that asked of him a king. And he said, This will be the manner of the king that shall reign over you: He will take your sons, and appoint them for himself, for his chariots, and to be his horsemen; and some shall run before his chariots. And he will appoint him captains over thousands, and captains over fifties; and will set them to ear his ground, and to reap his harvest, and to make his instruments of war, and instruments of his chariots. And he will take your daughters to be confectionaries, and to be cooks, and to be bakers. And he will take your fields, and your vineyards, and your oliveyards, even the best of them, and give them to his servants. And he will take the tenth of your seed, and of your vineyards, and give to

his officers, and to his servants. And he will take your menservants, and your maidservants, and your goodliest young men, and your asses, and put them to his work. He will take the tenth of your sheep: and ye shall be his servant. And ye shall cry out in that day because of your king which ye shall have chosen you; and the LORD will not hear you in that day.

"Nevertheless the people refused to obey the voice of Samuel; and they said, Nay; but we will have a king over us; That we also may be like all the nations; and that our king may judge us, and go out before us, and fight our battles. And Samuel heard all the words of the people, and he rehearsed them in the ears of the LORD. And the LORD said to Samuel, Hearken unto their voice, and make them a king" (1 Samuel 8:19-22).

The fact that David was left in office after committing adultery did not indicate God's approval of his sin. God did not ever approve of the position David held, much less of his sin.

(3) David was not a Christian. He belonged to the Jewish faith, which had entirely different rules about sex. Judaism said, "Thou shalt not commit adultery." Jesus said, "Ye have heard that it was said by them of old time, Thou shalt not commit adultery: But I say unto you, That whosoever looketh on a woman to lust after her hath committed adultery with her already in his heart" (Matthew 5:27,28). A clearly different and far higher code of morality is required of Christians than was required for David, a Jew. The Bible says: "Study to shew thyself approved unto God, a workman that needeth not to be ashamed, rightly dividing the word of truth (II Timothy 2:15). It is essential that we differentiate between the Old Testament laws for David and the New Testament require-

ments for Christians.

(4) The Holy Spirit's indwelling power was not given to men until the day of Pentecost. David did not have access to the power Christians have to overcome temptation and live holy. Jesus spoke of the Holy Spirit prior to dying on the cross and being resurrected: "But this spake he of the Spirit, which they that believe on him should receive: for the Holy Ghost was not yet given; because that Jesus was not yet glorified" (John 7:39). The conditions of salvation were the same before Pentecost, but the results of salvation were different. Christians receive a power to live holy—a power which was not available to David.

(5) David's doctrine of sexual morality assures the sexually immoral that their adultery will not send them to hell. It only deprives them of the joy of God's salvation: "Restore unto me the joy of thy salvation; and uphold me with thy free spirit" (Psalm 51:12). Sinners love this doctrine. If adultery fills the nights with boundless fun, who cares about losing a little divine joy?

It is a reasonable assumption that David was referring to his adultery in this Psalm. But it is only an assumption. To teach that David's cry for the restoration of joy was referring to adultery is teaching an assumption. There is no Scriptural proof of this. It would be just as reasonable to assume that David was talking about idolatry rather than adultery, for he said "against thee and thee only have I sinned" (Psalm 51:4). Certainly in the case of his adultery, he was sinning against Bathsheba and her husband.

(6) David did not just commit adultery with Bathsheba. He also became an accomplice in the murder of her husband. After he learned Bathsheba was pregnant, he ordered her husband to be killed in order to cover up his sin. Any attempt to minimize the evil of adultery, by means of Psalm 51, at the

same time attempts to minimize murder. If Clinton contracted the CIA to have a man killed, would the Clinton Clergymen be just as quick to say, "David had a man killed and God allowed him to continue as king. It couldn't be too bad?" And can you imagine a pastor preaching, "If you don't stop going around killing people you are going to lose the joy of your salvation"? David's story gives us no more reason to minimize adultery than it does to minimize murder. Yet, this is the interpretation given by those who wish to comfort adulterers.

SOFT PREACHING PRODUCES
A SEXUAL "KLEPTOMANIAC"

Bill Clinton has done what his ministers have taught him—treated sex as a very small matter. He moved in and lived with Hillary before they were married.[84] He confessed to committing adultery with Gennifer Flowers. Now, he has admitted to having an "improper relationship" with Monica Lewinsky, which was "wrong." DNA documents how wrong.

Paul Fick wrote in his book, *The Dysfunctional President*: "One of the more unseemly aspects of the Clinton character is his relentless sexual activity. Clinton's long-standing history of sexual liaisons throughout his marriage has resulted in scrutiny from a variety of sources....It is important to discuss Clinton's sexual liaisons because they exceed normal behavior and do affect his presidential activities. This sexual behavior most adequately can be described as pathological....People who have such problems spend an inordinate amount of time thinking about sexuality and engaging in sexually related activities."[85]

Fick points to the severity of the problem: "We are not observing a man who had an affair and is remorseful for hurting his spouse. We are observing an individual who is consumed with thoughts and behavior related to sex in much the same way that a drug abuser is consumed with thought and behaviors about his compulsion."[86]

Clinton's sexual behavior has become the laughing stock of the comedy world. Billy Crystal told the audience at the 1998 Academy Awards: "So much has changed in a year. A year ago the White House was complaining there was too much sex in *Hollywood.*" At last count, there were over 5,000 such jokes about the President's adultery.

The President exposed his throat to a pack of savage attackers when he engaged in bad sexual activity. A.M. Rosenthal, the highly respected *New York Times* editor and columnist, says, "For President Clinton to have illicit sex in the Oval Office would have been like doing it in Macy's window... and for him to take that risk could mean that he is obsessive, something like a sexual kleptomaniac."

How does the President deal with his sexual escapades? One of Clinton's favorite poems, Walt Whitman's *Leaves of Grass,* offers a clue. It says sex contains "all souls," "all gods" and "all justifications" for whatever deeds it may inspire:

Sex contains all,
Bodies, Souls, meanings, proofs, purities,
        delicacies, results, promulgations,
Songs, commands, health, pride, the maternal mystery,
        the seminal milk;
All hopes, benefactions, bestowals,
All the passions, loves, beauties, delights of the earth,
All the governments, judges, gods,
        follow'd persons of the earth,
These are contain'd in sex as parts of itself and
        justifications of itself.

Perhaps, in the eyes of Bill Clinton, the passion of sex did just that—justified itself.

CLINTON'S SPOKESPEOPLE
ECHO HIS VIEWS

The President's defenders have offered a view of adultery's innocence we must assume agrees with Clinton's beliefs, since he has never stopped them or corrected them. "It's about sex," pronounced Bill Press of *CNN's Crossfire*. "The one sort of lie that a civilized culture not only condones but depends upon [is] a consensual lie about consensual adultery."

David Frum says of the Bill Clinton generation, "But the central dogma of the baby boomers: the belief that sex, so long as it's consensual, ought never to be subject to moral scrutiny at all."

James Carville expressed his objection to moral scrutiny when he said: "These people are obsessed with sex. This thing is totally out of control....[Ken Starr is] a sex-obsessed person who's out to get the President....He's concerned about three things: sex, sex, and more sex." It may just be about sex, but in 1881 Judge E. J. Cox was impeached by the Minnesota legislature for "frequenting bawdy houses and consorting with harlots."[87]

"The only way to insist that adultery is intolerable while actually tolerating it is by hiding it in the closet....This is the real world, not *The Sound of Music*," writes Jonathan Rauch in the *National Journal*.

William J. Bennett says Clinton's defenders have reduced sex "to a mere riot of the glands." He cites Susan Estrich, the TV commentator, who excuses Clinton's adultery as nothing more than "finding comfort...in the arms of a beautiful twenty-one-year-old."

Nina Burleigh, a reporter for *Time* magazine, reflected the downplaying of adultery by saying, "I'd be happy to give him (oral sex) just to thank him for keeping abortion legal."

The White House has painted the President's critics as religious, right wing fanatics. But, in fact, even the religious right have had very little to say regarding Clinton's adultery. Ann Coulter complained about this, charging the "Christian Coalition hasn't made a peep about manifest perversions and apparent crimes, except to endorse the position of Clinton's flacks...it is just waiting 'to see the facts.' Be that as it may, surely it does not yet require fidelity to a particular religious creed to say the President of the United States should not be having affairs with an intern, lying to the American people, obstructing justice, or perjuring himself in a constitutional case."[88]

Clinton's crisis started with him finding comfort in the arms of a young woman. It is ending with him finding comfort in the arms of manipulative ministers.

WHAT THE CLINTON CLERGY SHOULD HAVE TOLD CLINTON ABOUT SEX

Clinton's Clergymen have grossly misrepresented the Bible's teaching regarding sex. God designed it: He knows the power of passion and says, "It is better to marry than to burn," or be on fire with desire. God is even for sex more than we are; He prescribes a year-long honeymoon for all newly-weds: "When a man hath taken a new wife, he shall not go out to war, neither shall he be charged with any business: but he shall be free at home one year, and shall cheer up his wife which he hath taken" (Deuteronomy 24:5).

The Biblical position on sex is to "be constantly ravished," but to keep it in the proper context of marriage. Sex is like fire. If it is in your heater or stove, it can serve you well and bring you much pleasure. But if fire gets in your walls, you've got problems. Likewise, sex contained in marriage can give you service and pleasure. But if it breaks out of the confines of marriage, it can be very destructive. Adultery kills marriages, threatens the future of children, and destroys the family, which is the foundation of society. So God holds a very strict position on where our sexual drive is to be released.

Bill Clinton's sexual problem is not just about what he has done, but it could also be about what he hasn't done. Scripture instructs: "Rejoice with the wife of thy youth. Let her be as the loving hind and pleasant roe; let her breasts satisfy thee at all times; and be thou ravished always with her love" (Proverbs 5:18,19).

Under the law God gave to the Jewish nation, sex outside of marriage was serious enough to demand the death penalty: "The man that committeth adultery with another man's wife, even he that committeth adultery with his neighbour's wife, the adulterer and the adulteress shall surely be put to death" (Leviticus 20:10-12).

Adultery made Jehovah God's list of deadly sins two times. The Ten Commandments say: "Thou shalt not commit adultery...thou shalt not covet thy neighbour's wife" (Exodus 20:14,17). Jesus Christ reiterated this: "Thou knowest the commandments, Do not commit adultery, Do not kill, Do not steal, Do not bear false witness, Defraud not, Honour thy father and mother" (Mark 10:19). And the Christian New Testament leaves no doubt about the fate of the immoral: "Marriage is honourable in all, and the bed undefiled: but whoremongers and adulterers God will judge" (Hebrews 13:4).

"Perjury and adultery by politicians are scandalous not because they give politicians a bad name, but because they give perjury and adultery a good one," says J. Budziszewski, a writer for *World* magazine..[89] This is exactly what the President's Prophets are doing—giving adultery a good name. In order to save Mr. Clinton's presidency, a tragic moral influence is being released upon a nation looking to the clergy for moral guidance.

To many people in the Clinton generation, sex is a very casual matter. His peers thought, and some still think, that sex is fun and funny. Now, as he crosses the 50-year mark, many still find Clinton's dilly-dallying with the girls to be entertaining. His adultery is the stuff our modern comedians joke about and cool audiences laugh about. But adultery is a tragedy. The Bible portrays just how tragic.

ADULTERY REDUCES
FREE PEOPLE TO SLAVES

Adultery controls people to the point they cannot stop: "Having eyes full of adultery, and that cannot cease from sin; beguiling unstable souls" (II Peter 2:14).

It has the power enslave men and women to the point that that they have no more control of their passions than an animal: "They...committed adultery, and assembled themselves by troops in the harlots' houses. They were as fed horses in the morning: every one neighed after his neighbour's wife" (Jeremiah 5:7,8).

Adultery has the power to lead a man into depths of indecency: "For of this sort are they which creep into houses, and lead captive silly women laden with sins, led away with divers lusts" (II Timothy 3:6).

It is hard for the public to realize that a man as powerful as Bill Clinton could be reduced to a mere slave of lust. But as Dr. Jerome Levin explains, "Powerful, mysterious Eros, the Greek god of erotic love, demands worship. To withhold it, the fable goes, is to miss a fulfilled life. Yet to yield can mean becoming his slave." He adds, "Sexual addiction is worship without restraint—worship that results in bondage and loss of self. This is no less true for the king than for the beggar."[90]

Dr. Levin explains the power of sex to enslave like this, "Sexual addiction, like all forms of addiction, is a form of slavery. Addicts are, in essence, slaves to their addictions because the addictions take over their lives to the point where they feel powerless to stop the behavior and also lose their authority and freedom of choice in all areas of life. Therefore, because of the enslaving nature of addictions, addicts are able to avoid or flee from the responsibilities that come with freedom.[91] Mr. Clinton's office has bestowed on him the power to command a nuclear arsenal that could blow up the world. It cannot give him the power to say "no" to lust.

THE TREMENDOUS COST OF
ADULTERY HERE AND NOW

Adultery destroys mighty rulers: "Give not thy strength unto women, nor thy ways to that which destroyeth kings" (Proverbs 31:3). Mark Anthony's lust for Cleopatra cost him the Roman Empire. Charles Stewart Parnell's passion for Kitty O'Shea cost the Irish their strongest leader and could well have delayed their liberation from English rule for a generation. Clinton's lust has cost him the influence of the most powerful position on earth.

People familiar with the Bible are not surprised that Mr. Clinton has been so careless in his sexual misconduct. The Bible teaches that sex deceives people into thinking they will not be caught: "The eye also of the adulterer waiteth for the twilight, saying, No eye shall see me: and disguiseth his face. In the dark they dig through houses, which they had marked for themselves in the daytime: they know not the light" (Job

24:15). Clinton has functioned as a man who thinks he is beyond the danger of being found out.

The tragic loss of respect, the expensive legal bills and the unremovable reproach President Clinton faces were predictable. The Bible warns: "But whoso committeth adultery with a woman lacketh understanding: he that doeth it destroyeth his own soul. A wound and dishonour shall he get; and his reproach shall not be wiped away" (Proverbs 6:32,33).

Andy Rooney, in an editorial titled, "Clinton's future: Hell on earth, joke for posterity," says, "The Clinton sex scandal is one of the tawdriest stories ever to become public, and the history books will never forget it. If there are people on Earth a thousand years from now, they'll read about it. How would you like facing posterity with that on your record?"[92] He adds, "The life Bill Clinton has ahead of him will be hell. He will be able to make money just going around being Bill Clinton in front of large audiences who will pay to see and hear him as a curiosity, but he will forever be a disgraced president. It will be the biggest thing on his mind every morning when he wakes up and before he goes to sleep at night. And during those terrible middle-of-the-nights."[93] As the Scripture says, "his reproach shall not be wiped away."

Actually Bill Clinton should not be too flattered by the attention of women. He represents only one thing to them, a nice trophy to hang on the wall and show off. The Bible says, just as a deer hunter waits for his prey to appear: "My son...a whore is a deep ditch, and a strange woman is a narrow pit. She also lieth in wait as for a prey, and increaseth the transgressors among men" (Proverbs 23:26-28). Such women have no more affection for the man than the hunter does for the deer. They just want a new trophy on the wall. The more important, rich, or powerful the man, the more valuable the trophy. This is why rulers, rock stars, and prominent athletes are valued prey: "The adulteress will hunt for the precious life" (Proverbs 6:26).

In a graphic foreshadowing of the Clinton situation, the Scripture says: "For the lips of a strange woman drop as an honeycomb, and her mouth is smoother than oil: But her end is bitter as wormwood, sharp as a two edged sword....Remove thy way far from her, and come not nigh the door of her house: Lest thou give thine honour unto others, and thy years unto the cruel: Lest strangers be filled with thy wealth" (Proverbs 5:3,4,8-10). And so, the honor of the Clinton presidency has been taken away. It hangs as a trophy on the walls of wayward women. The wealth of the president has also been taken away. It is in the pockets of his lawyers.

There is nothing surprising about the President having spent years without any apparent guilt or remorse about his adultery. The Bible declares: "Such is the way of an adulterous woman; she eateth, and wipeth her mouth, and saith, I have done no wickedness" (Proverbs 30:20). Adultery murders the conscience. People find that after several times, they feel no more guilt, no more remorse and no more urgency about ceasing.

THE EXPENSE OF ADULTERY
IN THE WORLD TO COME

The Bible explicitly says adulterers cannot enter heaven: "For this ye know, that no whoremonger, nor unclean person, nor covetous man, who is an idolater, hath any inheritance in the kingdom of Christ and of God. Let no man deceive you with vain words: for because of these things cometh the wrath of God upon the children of disobedience" (Ephesians 5:5,6). Clinton succumbed to the cunning words of deceitful preachers who did not make it plain that adulterers cannot enter heaven.

Again the Scripture is emphatic at this point: "Now the works of the flesh are manifest, which are these; Adultery, fornication, uncleanness, lasciviousness...Envyings, murders, drunkenness, revellings, and such like: of the which I tell you before, as I have also told you in time past, that they which do such things shall not inherit the kingdom of God" (Galatians 5:19,21).

God says that fornicators or adulterers who think they are going to heaven have been deceived: "Know ye not that the unrighteous shall not inherit the kingdom of God? Be not deceived: neither fornicators, nor idolaters, nor adulterers, nor effeminate, nor abusers of themselves with mankind, Nor thieves, nor covetous, nor drunkards, nor revilers, nor extortioners, shall inherit the kingdom of God. And such were some of you: but ye are washed, but ye are sanctified, but ye are justified in the name of the Lord Jesus, and by the Spirit of our God" (I Corinthians 6:9,11). Paul assures those who "were" living in these sins, but who have turned from them to Christ, that they are now "justified" in the eyes of God.

God's Word warns that by choosing to live in sexual immorality, a person also chooses its horrid consequence of going into eternal fire and brimstone: "But the fearful, and unbelieving, and the abominable, and murderers, and whoremongers, and sorcerers, and idolaters, and all liars, shall have their part in the lake which burneth with fire and brimstone: which is the second death" (Revelation 21:8).

SEX IS THE SAME
AS "SHAKING HANDS"

I was in San Francisco in the 60's when the American sex revolution burst into flames that would sweep across our nation. In an unprecedented moment, America radically changed its moral values more quickly and drastically than any nation in history. One day as I walked through the historic Haight Ashbury section with my Bible, an angry 18-year-old girl lashed out at me. "The trouble with all you old, straight people is you don't understand sex," she shouted. "When you meet, you shake hands. When we meet, we have sex. There is no difference between sex and shaking hands," she boldly declared. Today, the moral philosophy of a 60's street hippie, has made it all the way to the White House.

Cal Thomas says, "Mr. Clinton feels about religion the way he feels about sex. He likes the kind that makes him feel good but requires nothing of him. That's why some of his best friends are the liberal clergy who cloak him with the mantle of respectability even while he lives and lies as he pleases."[94]

But the clergymen's cloak of respectability is being ripped apart. It reveals that adultery is very serious. It has devastated Clinton's family, embarrassed his daughter, disrupted his government, destroyed the legacy of his presidency and misdirected the morals of a whole generation of children. All this, when it was "just about sex," as Rev. Jesse Jackson says.

Chapter Six

WHO IS GOING TO CAST THE FIRST STONE?

Throughout President Clinton's life he has heard ministers preach "judge not." The moment his moral failure became public, they exploded into a chorus of religious voices erupting across the air waves: "Don't judge the President." "Judge not." "Who are we to judge?" "Judge not that ye be not judged." Rev. Jesse Jackson says, "Let him that is without sin cast the first stone." Yet Rev. Jackson has not hesitated to stone Kenneth Starr. He has even called him a "snake." The minister called to the White House for spiritual counsel has sought to give comfort to the Clintons and discomfort to Kenneth Starr. "It was when Adam and Eve ate the forbidden fruit," Jackson explained, that all the cover-ups started. "The moral here is, 'You should have stopped talking to the snake in the first place.'"[95] This means Clinton never should have talked to Kenneth Starr—or the "snake."

Along with Jesse Jackson, other Clinton team members have thrown enough rocks at Kenneth Starr to build a pyramid. James Carville, the President's number-one stone thrower, says of Starr: "I just flat out do not like him. I think he's an abusive, privacy-invading, sex-obsessed, right-wing, constitutionally insensitive, boring, obsequious, and miserable little man who has risen further in this life by his willingness to suck up to power than his meager talents and pitiful judgment ever would have gotten him...you'll never catch me shaking hands with him." The Clinton Clergymen have used the Bible to declare we shouldn't judge and yet they have turned right around and judged the Special Prosecutor.

These Scripture quotes have obviously been used to try and stop the criticism of Bill Clinton and to protect his presidency. Ironically, instead of protecting him, these comments may have compounded the President's troubles and played a part in his moral disgrace.

THE ERRONEOUS TEACHING
ON JUDGING

In an *Atlanta Constitution Journal* article titled "Crisis in the White House Clerics Reluctant to Cast First Stone at President," Julia Malone writes about all the ministers who try to stop people from judging the President. "I would just say don't rush to judgment," said the Rev. Philip Wogaman. The Methodist pastor said on *ABC's Nightline*, "He's a man of great depth and vitality and service to the country. If there are problems, then perhaps he needs counsel." Wogaman added that "there have been some very fine people, including Dr. Martin Luther King, who've had problems of this sort." And of course no one would dare to "judge" Dr. Martin Luther King.[96] There is no more pervasive, destructive error within the Christian church than the idea that members are forbidden to say that anybody or anything is wrong.

Ministerial misinterpretation of Jesus' teaching on judging have hurt the President in two ways. First, it has stopped Christians from giving the President strong rebukes that might have awakened him. Second, it has made Clinton look upon anyone who has attempted to correct him as being judgmental. And any person who is judgmental, his reasoning goes, is disobeying Jesus and a hypocrite. This perversion of a Bible truth has been used to turn those with Christian concern for the President into enemies. In this way, Mr. Clinton has been put beyond the help of those with the courage to rebuke him. President Clinton might have seen those who called for him to repent as benefactors, heeded their call, and avoided his troubles if only his clergymen had told him the truth about judging.

WHAT THE BIBLE ACTUALLY
TEACHES ABOUT JUDGING

The Biblical word "judge" has more than one meaning, just as the word "gay" can either mean "a happy person," or "a homosexual." The word "judge" can either mean "to condemn a person to harsh penalty" or it can mean "to simply decide if someone is right or wrong."

The Greek word translated "judge" in the English Bible is *krino*.[97] It means: "to distinguish, i.e. decide (mentally or judicially); by implication, to try, condemn, punish." In the King James version of the Bible it is used in varied ways: avenge, conclude, condemn, damn, decree, determine, esteem, judge, go to (sue at the) law, ordain, call in question, sentence to, think. The definitions can vary from "decide" to "damn."

When Jesus, in Matthew 7:1, said we are not to judge, He meant we are not to "damn," or say "that person should be put in hell." But He by no means prohibits us from "deciding" which people are good and which are bad. In the very same passage, He tells us to "give not that which is holy unto the dogs, neither cast ye your pearls before swine" (Matthew 7:6). This demands that we "decide" who is a "dog" and who is a "swine."

Jesus meant we should not "damn, condemn, or punish." I am disobeying Jesus when I say, "my neighbor is an offensive drunk and I hope lightening strikes him dead." It would also be breaking this command to say, "My no-good, drug-abusing neighbor who beats his wife should be in jail or in hell." If I do this I am judging him in the sense of "condemnation."

On the other hand, when Jesus said in John 7:24 to "Judge not according to the appearance, but judge righteous judgment," He means for us "to decide" whether the neighbor is doing something wrong. This also means that I should point out to my children that they should not use drugs and behave like the neighbor. It also means I should pray for my neighbor and do everything I can to help him get off drugs and stop his abusive practices.

It has been said that all heresy is just truth stretched out of proportion. The Clinton Clergymen have stretched "judging" to a preposterous meaning. We should not consign people to hell, but we should judge that adultery and lying are bad actions that should be dealt with.

Christ's command against judging does not mean we are to refrain from distinguishing right from wrong. This is apparent in Luke 12:57 when Jesus asked, "Why even of yourselves judge ye not what is right?" Just as the Bible teaches us not to "condemn" or "publish" others, it also teaches us to "decide" issues of right and wrong: "Do ye not know that the saints shall judge the world? and if the world shall be judged by you, are ye unworthy to judge the smallest matters?" (I Corinthians 6:2,3); "I speak as to wise men; judge ye what I say" (I Corinthians 10:15).

Jesse Jackson and the others screaming against judging the President should remember that all judging does not conclude a person is guilty of wrongdoing. Sometimes judging proves a man is guiltless and good. So when the Clinton Clergy say, "The President has done a good job of running the economy," they are judging the man. When Rev. Bill Hybels, pastor of the huge Willow Creek Church near Chicago, praised the President at his 1996 inauguration, there was no protest about his positive judgment. According to *World* magazine, Hybels applauded Mr. Clinton for, "the wisdom and leadership and the vision in your life the past four years." He lauded, "the development of your heart, your increasing desire to know God, and to live for Him..." Hybels said he wanted Mr. Clinton to know "to the depths of your being that you are loved by many, many of us." If it is disobeying Scripture to judge that Bill Clinton is doing a terrible job as a husband, father and setting a bad example to the nation, it is just as wrong to judge that Bill Clinton is doing a good job with the economy, the social security and the welfare. Judging works both ways.

"Now the nation has to decide whether it is willing to be led by a repentant sinner. That will be a journey for the nation and not just for the President," declared Rev. Dr. Joan B. Campbell, General Secretary of the National Council of Churches. After listening to President Clinton speak at the White House Interfaith Prayer Breakfast, Campbell pronounced that Clinton, "is now repentant. He offered a much fuller statement, a truly confessional statement with a religious character to it, and asked the forgiveness of the nation, his family, his colleagues and of Monica Lewinsky and her family. He talked about the need for repentance, for a turning around, for a new direction, his need to find that new direction in his life, and what a spiritual journey it's been for him. This prayer breakfast was a religious event in the best sense of the word, not just people saying prayers, but an event with a prayerful quality about it." Dr. Campbell thanked President Clinton "for being honest and willing to be vulnerable. It's not easy for powerful people to be vulnerable."[98] Here Rev. Campbell has judged the President. Based on listening to him talk, she has decided he is now repentant. Right or wrong, she has judged him and the verdict is positive. But it is no less "judging" than when someone says Clinton is not repentant.

If the Presidential Prophets had been accurately teaching the Bible, they would have cried to the American public, "Judge righteous judgment." Then Congress and the American people would have been admonished to be fair in considering the evidence against the President and come to a "righteous" conclusion.

FALSE TEACHING ABOUT "CASTING THE FIRST STONE"

The Presidential Prophets are again twisting the Scripture when they talk about "casting the first stone." When the ungodly Pharisees asked Jesus if a woman whom they had caught in the act of adultery should be stoned to death, Jesus replied, "He that is without sin among you, let him first cast a stone at her" (John 8:7) This resulted in the woman's accusers being convicted of their own misdeeds, walking away and leaving the two alone in the temple. The grateful, contrite woman declared Jesus her "Lord." Then Christ said, "Neither do I condemn thee: go, and sin no more" (John 8:11). This shows us that God forgives repentant sinners when they are willing for Him to be their "Lord," or "Master." The story also stresses that individuals do not have a right to take the law into their own hands and kill people. Even if our neighbor is a drug user and wife abuser, we should not go over and stone him to death.

In a clever way, Christ dispersed the woman's accusing mob when He said, "Let him that is without sin cast the first stone." However, had there been one without sin, the woman still should not have been murdered. This Biblical passage brings home the truth that individuals should not stone other individuals to death. There is not a word in this passage condemning individuals for criticizing the conduct of other individuals. Christ himself judged the woman's sin so bad that she must "go and sin no more."

By insulating the President from people "judging righteous judgments" about his conduct and from people who in the name of God would "rebuke him sharply," the Clinton Clergy have deprived the President of divinely ordained help that might have saved him from his moral muddle.

Chapter Seven

STRAIGHT IS SIN, BUT ORAL IS OKAY

Jennifer Flowers, the woman President Clinton confessed to having a sexual relationship with, has said Clinton told her he had found in the Bible that oral sex is all right. Even though Flowers was willing to have a 10 year sexual relationship with Mr. Clinton, she told him, "I'm not going there."[99] Unlike Clinton, Flowers could handle adultery, but not oral sex. Sexual perversion was too much for her. She explained the President had the ability to convince himself that a thing was true. She believed he really was convinced that oral sex is all right and that the Bible supports his position.

Dr. Jerome Levin echoed Jennifer's statement when he said, "Clinton is said to have used religion to excuse certain behaviors. He reportedly confided in a friend that oral sex must be okay because the Bible does not regard it as adultery. Some commentators have anticipated that Clinton's denial of having sexual relationships with various women, including Monica Lewinsky, will be defended by his assertion that oral sex is somehow different from a *sexual relationship*."[100] Martin Luther, the German reformer, would have agreed with Lewinsky's and Levin's assessment. He said, "The ultimate proof of the sinner is that he does not know his own sin." Clinton, by engaging in oral sex, has blinded his eyes to the fact that it is a sin.

Jennifer Flower's revelation that Clinton believes the Bible allows oral sex could explain two things: (1) The report that Clinton refused Monica Lewinsky's request for natural sex, and (2) why he strongly supports homosexuals. If the Bible approves of oral sex, homosexuals are righteous virgins.

CLERGYMAN PROCLAIMS THAT
UNNATURAL SEX IS APPROVED BY GOD

In 1995, Rev. Philip Wogaman told the homosexual newspaper, *Washington Blade,* "I want to emphasize that I honor the number of people in our congregation who are gay who are in deeply committed relationships. I have found many examples of love which I find deeply moving."[101] A year later he repeated this message to the United Methodist's General Conference.

Rev. Wogaman is an outspoken advocate of homosexual marriages. After Rev. Kwabena Rainey Creech, the pastor of Omaha's largest United Methodist Church, was suspended from the leadership of his congregation on November 10, 1998 for performing a homosexual wedding, Wogaman said, "We have to find a way to be supportive of these committed relationships. The church also speaks in many voices."[102]

Mark Tooley, a Methodist who works at the Washington, D.C. Institute on Religion and Democracy, has documented how deeply Wogaman and his church have plunged into their support of sexual perversion. Tooley said a homosexuality symposium at Foundry United Methodist Church in Washington, D. C., featured ridicule of the Christian Nativity story, questions about portraying Jesus as a drag queen, praise for homosexual marriage, and a declaration that the Ten Commandments are immoral. The keynote speaker was Episcopal Bishop John Spong, who has defied his Episcopal denomination by ordaining homosexual priests. Tooley says, "The day-long 'celebration' was organized by PFLAG (Parents, Families and Friends of Lesbians and Gays). The...symposium, called 'Sharing Our Rainbow of Light,' surprised even their mostly homosexual audience of several hundred persons with their denial of traditional religious beliefs."[103]

Tooley reported: "The homosexual symposium...was concluded with an ecumenical worship service involving numerous clergy, including a Washington Catholic priest who announced he had recently 'come out publicly.' One worship leader identified herself as a 'lesbian Unitarian.' The Rev. Cheeks of the Inner Light Unity Fellowship, a New Age group, prayed to 'ancestors, lights, angels, saints and spirits of Buddha, Mohammed and Jesus.' United Methodist minister Harry Kieley declared, 'Jesus is speaking as a gay man to the church today. The United Methodist Church has been supporting the persecution of human beings (homosexuals?)."[104]

Episcopal Bishop Sprong, realizing that God and the Bible are opposed to any sexual deviation, launched a blatant attack on the Scripture. He said, "Every image of God is mythological." Sprong declared the resurrection and virgin birth of Jesus did not actually happen and that Jesus' earthly father Joseph, the disciples, and Judas are fictional characters whom the early church created. Bishop Sprong said the apostle Paul was a homosexual: "Our primary understanding of God's grace came from a self-hating, gay man." The bishop said forcing the church to legitimize homosexuality is "a total justice issue exactly like the civil rights movement....Asked about the possibility of Jesus Christ being depicted in art as a 'drag queen,' Wogaman replied, 'I don't condemn it. I just don't know. I'll have to think about it some more.'"[105]

When Mark Tooley and Cal Thomas wrote editorials criticizing Wogaman's anti-Biblical position, Clinton's pastor responded by linking them to the Oklahoma bomber and saying they were just out to get the President. "People in the media don't plant bombs," he wrote. "But if they plant hatred and division, doesn't that affect the behavior of unstable hearers or readers?" Wogaman declared, "I think much of this was a political attack aimed at getting at President Clinton through the practice of his religion."

Despite Wogaman's efforts to include homosexuals and the attraction of "the President's church," membership and attendance have fallen more than ten percent since Wogaman became pastor. Tooley says, "Most of Foundry's liberal neighbors are more inclined to attend the Broadway shows regularly produced in the church's fellowship hall than attend the Sunday sermons. Tolerance of unbiblical teachings, abortion and homosexuality has paralleled Methodism's drastic decline. It was once America's largest denomination. Today it is America's fastest declining denomination."[106] And it is not just Methodism. As pastors abandon the preaching of God's Word, their churches have no reason to exist. They decline and die. George Barna, a religious researcher and president of Barna Research Group, reports the average weekly adult attendance at Protestant churches has declined by 9 percent in the past year. The average operating budget declined 15 percent, from $123,000 to $105,000.[107]

CLINTON GOES WITH HIS CLERGYMEN

Tragically, President Clinton has not joined the numbers dropping out of a church that is attacking the Christian faith instead of teaching it. He has continued to sit under unbiblical teachings about sex. The results have been pro-homosexual legislation and a sexually deviant life.

On May 28, 1998 President Clinton issued an Executive Order that added homosexuals to the classes of federal workers protected from discrimination. Even House Democratic Leader Richard Gephardt (D-Mo.), disagreed with the President, saying: "Sexual orientation should not be considered in the hiring, promoting, or terminating of an employee in the federal government. You would think that this would be something we could all agree on." "The White House," said Representative Joseph Pitts (R-Pa.), "is promoting an extremely special interest position. President Clinton was out of step with the majority of Americans who oppose quotas based on one's behavior or lifestyle."

Clinton, a child of the 60's, lives out its defining theme, "Make love, not war." Now, he is learning the shame and hurt of unbounded license that the 60's hippies refused to see. Tragically President Clinton does not reap the entire harvest for his deeds. The children of America are suffering for one man's adultery. In addition to legislation supporting homosexuality, Clinton has given children a role model of perversion.

Ann Coulter commented on the President's deviate practices, "To paraphrase the current 'just about sex' line, Watergate was about a two-bit breaking and entering. And unlike with Monica Lewinsky, it wasn't committed by the president, or even by people who worked at his White House, but by people who worked for his campaign committee. Grand-sounding treacheries weren't required by the framers, weren't required for Nixon, and aren't required now. It's enough for the president to be a pervert."[108]

An *AP Report* begins: "World War II, Mc-Carthyism, Space Exploration, those are the things high schoolers usually talk about. In Betsy Grady's Modern History class, Friday's topic was straight out of the tabloids: the sex life of a sitting president. The discussions here and elsewhere are making some parents and teachers so uncomfortable that the students are taking reports of the President's alleged sexual escapades with a 21 year-old intern with more cynicism and resignation than surprise. 'It seems like this has been a pattern' said Betsy, a 10th grader at the Cambridge Latin School, 'maybe this is just who he is.' 'An open season debate on the President's sex life upon school children is unprecedented' said Grady, age 51. But some of the fifteen public school students slouched in their chairs seemed aware that their lesson was out of the ordinary. While some teachers, like Grady, feel comfortable with open discussions that occasionally prompt some outburst of questionable taste from the students, others feel ill at ease with the issues. What do you do when a kid asks, 'What's oral sex?' a teacher wondered. 'We don't know what to tell them.'"

WHAT THE BIBLE TEACHES ABOUT
ORAL AND ANAL INTERCOURSE

Had President Clinton's Clergymen been honest, they would have taught him what the Bible actually says about sexual deviance. Homosexuality got its legal and proper name—sodomy—from a militant group of men who adamantly refused an offer of natural sex with girls and demanded unnatural sex with men:

> "And they called unto Lot, and said unto him, Where are the men which came in to thee this night? bring them out unto us, that we may know them. And Lot went out at the door unto them, and shut the door after him, And said, I pray you, brethren, do not so wickedly. Behold now, I have two daughters which have not known man; let me, I pray you, bring them out unto you, and do ye to them as is good in your eyes: only unto these men do nothing; for therefore came they under the shadow of my roof. And they said, Stand back. And they said again, This one fellow came in to sojourn, and he will needs be a judge: now will we deal worse with thee, than with them. And they pressed sore upon the man, even Lot, and came near to break the door" (Genesis 19:5-9).

Sodom's militant homosexuality led to its destruction: "Even as Sodom and Gomorrah, and the cities about them in like manner, giving themselves over to fornication, and going after strange flesh, are set forth for an example, suffering the vengeance of eternal fire" (Jude 1:7). And so the center of militant, flagrant, homosexual conduct was immortalized in giving the name of "sodomy" to oral and anal intercourse.

The Hebrew word for a "sodomite" is *arsenokoites* (ar-sen-ok-oy'-tace); (*Strong's Greek and Hebrew Dictionary* says it is used as "abuser of (that defile self) with mankind; growth (by germination or expansion), i.e. (by implication) natural production (lineal descent)." Any sex that does not produce "natural production or lineal descent," would fit under the definition of sodomy.[109]

Perversion, or unnatural sex, includes sex with an animal: "Thou shalt not lie with mankind, as with womankind: it is abomination. Neither shalt thou lie with any beast to defile thyself therewith: neither shall any woman stand before a beast to lie down thereto: it is confusion" (Leviticus 18:22,23).

In the Christian New Testament, sodomy includes any "unnatural sex:" "Wherefore God also gave them up to uncleanness through the lusts of their own hearts, to dishonour their own bodies between themselves....For this cause God gave them up unto vile affections: for even their women did change the natural use into that which is against nature: And likewise also the men, leaving the natural use of the woman, burned in their lust one toward another; men with men working that which is unseemly, and receiving in themselves that recompense of their error which was meet" (Romans 1:24,26,27). The passage speaks of men who "put aside the natural use of the woman." This condemns unnatural oral and anal intercourse with a mate, as well as all sex with a partner of the same gender.

God demonstrated his strong opposition to sexual deviation by ordering the Jewish nation to put sodomites out of the country: "There shall be no whore of the daughters of Israel, nor a sodomite of the sons of Israel" (Deuteronomy 23:17).

People practicing sodomy are on God's list of the lawless, disobedient, ungodly, sinners: "Knowing this, that the law is not made for a righteous man, but for the lawless and disobedient, for the ungodly and for sinners...For whoremongers, for them that defile themselves with mankind, for menstealers, for liars, for perjured persons, and if there be any other thing that is contrary to sound doctrine; for menstealers, for liars, for perjured persons, and if there be any other thing that is contrary to sound doctrine" (I Timothy 1:9,10).

Again, God says people who practice fornicating before they marry, people who practice adultery after they are married, and those who practice sexual deviations will not enter the kingdom of heaven: "Know ye not that the unrighteous shall not inherit the kingdom of God? Be not deceived: neither fornicators, nor idolaters, nor adulterers, nor effeminate, nor abusers of themselves with mankind (*"arsenokoites,"* the word *Strong's Greek and Hebrew Dictionary* defines as a "sodomite")" (I Corinthians 6:9).

A study of 7,500 homosexual obituaries reveals one reason God is so opposed to homosexuality; they only live about half as long as heterosexuals. This study by researchers of the Family Research Institute in Washington, D.C., reveals that, "the average age of death for a homosexual is forty-one. Lesbians live, on the average, to the age of forty-four." Institute Chairman, Paul Cameron, who led the study said, "It appears that homosexuals not only live markedly shorter lives today, but upon review of the scientific literature over the past 140 years, it looks like few homosexuals achieved old age in the past." Why? The study shows, "Homosexuals have a much higher rate of suicide, murder, accidents and, most important, disease. Homosexuality reduces life expectancy far more than smoking, drinking, or using drugs."[110]

Possibly, if Clinton had been taught the Bible truths about sexual deviance, he would have understood the Bible does condemn oral sex. Since the President reportedly refrained from natural sex with Miss Lewinsky because he understood this to be wrong, there is the possibility he would have refrained from deviate sexual involvement with her, had his ministers taught him that perversion is also wrong. And Clinton's Clergymen could have possibly prevented this whole dark tragedy had they convinced him of this one Bible truth: "The mouth of strange women is a deep pit: he that is abhorred of the LORD shall fall therein" (Proverbs 22:14).

Chapter Eight

MORALLY, WE ARE ALL THE SAME

Clinton is "only guilty of being like the rest of us, in that we are not perfect," declares Rev. Chandler D. Owens, Atlanta's presiding bishop of the Church of God in Christ. "I'm in the business of saving sin-sick souls. I believe the human personality is worth more than to be destroyed over these kinds of things," the bishop said. In a letter to the President, Owens offered "prayerful support during what must be a difficult time" and suggested that he focus on doing the larger good for the country. He pointed to the Bible's call for people to pray for their leaders:" "I will therefore that men pray every where, lifting up holy hands, without wrath and doubting" (I Timothy 2:8).

"We are not perfect," is a correct, but misleading statement aimed at taking away the right of anyone to criticize the President. It can appear to make all men moral equals. This is what Rev. Owens shamelessly stated, Clinton is "guilty of being like the rest of us." So Clinton is no better or worse than we are! Cal Thomas says the President is trying to create a doctrine of "immoral equivalency." By exposing the scandals of others, like Rep. Dan Burton for illegitimate parenting, they create the impression that we are all equally sinners. Thomas says, "How quickly we've regressed from Richard Nixon's 'I'm not a crook' to Bill Clinton's 'Hey, we're all crooks.'"[111]

On the *Today Show* Rev. Billy Graham echoed this idea. When Katie Couric asked him about his relationships with Bill Clinton and Richard Nixon. Graham replied, "I respect him. Because each man has his failures, and none of us are perfect. And Jesus said, 'He that is without sin among you, let him cast the first stone.'" Of course, the woman in Graham's stoning reference was converted to Christ, who demanded that she start living a new life unequal to her past life—"go and sin no more."

Rev. J. Philip Wogaman, Clinton's Washington pastor, continued building on the moral equivalence theme. Following the 1998 White House prayer breakfast, he told his congregation to examine their own sins and "foolish ways" and "seek mercy" themselves. Pressing for people to forgive the President and allow him to continue in office, Wogaman said, "Which of these defines the soul of America: the way of repentance and forgiveness, or the way of judgment? Where are we as a people?" Wogaman asked.[112]

The point the Clinton Clergy repeatedly makes is that there is really no difference in Bill Clinton and any other human being. We are all morally equal. The logical conclusion they would lead us to is there should be no criticism and certainly no removal from office. Tragically, their efforts to help Mr. Clinton are actually extremely harmful to him. It convinces him there is no opportunity for a life that is morally superior to his, since we are all alike sinners—all morally equal. The natural conclusion of this reasoning is that Mr. Clinton should not hope to overcome adultery, lying are any other sins. We all live and die moral equals.

Experience and Holy Scripture agree that we are all sinners—none of us is perfect. However, we are not all morally equal. If we are all morally equal why are some of us in prison while others are on the outside? Why do we have police and judges if we are all morally equal? How can one person arrest another, or judge another, if all are equal? Our whole judicial system is based on the fact that some people are morally inferior to others.

Scripture, like experience, says "all have sinned," but it refutes the conclusion that we are all morally equal. The purpose of Jesus Christ coming into this world was to make his disciples unequal—morally different: "blameless and harmless, the sons of God, without rebuke, in the midst of a crooked and perverse nation, among whom ye shine as lights in the world" (Philippians 2:15). This is the business of Christianity, producing people who will bring glory to God by being conspicuously different.

A converted Christians is morally different from other people for four reasons:

1. THEY POSSESS A GOD-GIVEN PASSION TO LIVE A HOLY LIFE

Genuine Christians possess a deep desire to overcome their dark passions and live a righteous life: "Blessed are they which do hunger and thirst after righteousness: for they shall be filled" (Matthew 5:6). The apostle Paul, who had been a persecutor and killer of Christians, received this passion for perfection when he was converted: "Not as though I had already attained, either were already perfect: but I follow after, if that I may apprehend that for which also I am apprehended of Christ Jesus...but this one thing I do, forgetting those things which are behind, and reaching forth unto those things which are before, I press toward the mark for the prize of the high calling of God in Christ Jesus. Let us therefore, as many as be perfect (consecrated) be thus minded" (Phillipians 3:12-15).

Paul shared his passion: "Having therefore these promises, dearly beloved, let us cleanse ourselves from all filthiness of the flesh and spirit, perfecting holiness in the fear of God" (II Corinthians 7:1). Paul hungered and thirsted for perfection as much as Bill Clinton hungered to be president.

2. THEY HAVE SUPERNATURAL POWER TO OVERCOME TEMPTAION

True Christians are morally different because they have Christ's Spirit living inside their bodies. True conversion means a person receives God's power to overcome the lusts like those that have assailed President Clinton: "Grace and peace be multiplied unto you through the knowledge of God, and of Jesus our Lord, According as his divine power hath given unto us all things that pertain unto life and godliness...Whereby are given unto us exceeding great and precious promises: that by these ye might be partakers of the divine nature, having escaped the corruption that is in the world through lust" (II Peter 1:2-4).

God works in the life of genuine Christians to strengthen them and make them perfect, or mature: "But the God of all grace, who hath called us unto his eternal glory by Christ Jesus, after that ye have suffered a while, make you perfect, stablish, strengthen, settle you" (I Peter 5:10).

Again, the Bible explains that the Holy Spirit produces the fruit of righteousness in the believer as naturally as a pear tree produces pears: "but the fruit of the Spirit is love, joy, peace, long-suffering, gentleness, goodness, faith, meekness, temperance" (Galatians 5:22,23).

3. CHRISTIANS ARE CHASTISED
OUT OF THEIR SINS

God's children are morally different because they are chastened when they are bad. President Clinton, despite his lying and immorality, is enjoying tremendous good fortune. He holds the biggest job on the planet. His job approval rating is good. The nation's finances and employment rates are great. He is popular—pulling high numbers in the polls. An Arab terrorist's plot to kill him was thwarted. Everything is going fantastic for him.

Here is the problem with all Clinton's good fortune. The Bible says God whips his children when they are bad: "For whom the Lord loveth he chasteneth, and scourgeth every son whom he receiveth. If ye endure chastening, God dealeth with you as with sons; for what son is he whom the father chasteneth not? But if ye be without chastisement, whereof all are partakers, then are ye bastards, and not sons....Now no chastening for the present seemeth to be joyous, but grievous: nevertheless afterward it yieldeth the peaceable fruit of righteousness unto them which are exercised thereby" (Hebrews 12:6-8). Chastisements are exclusive. They are reserved only for His true children. Anyone professing to be a Christian who is not chastened when they persist in sin, is illegitimate. The church may be their mother, but God is not their father.

God does not tolerate continual immorality in His children. He whips them in line. The Psalmist said, "Thou in faithfulness hath afflicted me" (Psalm 119:75). Chastening proves the faithfulness of our Heavenly Father to an earthly child. God's chastisement assures us of God's delight "in" us. Proverbs 3:12 says, "For whom the Lord loveth he corrected;

even as a father the son in whom he delighteth." When we are chastened we are reassured that our Heavenly Father looks upon us with the special fondness only shown to His children.

Christians in the early church at Corinth received assurance of their salvation in a painful way. After being "called to be saints" (I Corinthians 1:2), their moral conduct became shameful. The Scripture says, "For this cause many are weak and sickly among you...For...we are chastened of the Lord, that we should not be condemned with the world" (I Corinthians 11:30-32). The fact that the President has not been chastened, but rather blessed with great success, offers an alarming prospect for his eternal future.

What happens when Christians are chastised and still do not repent? There are sins a Christian "brother" can commit that will cost him his life: "If any man see his brother sin a sin which is not unto death, he shall ask, and he shall give him life for them that sin not unto death. There is a sin unto death: I do not say that he shall pray for it" (I John 5:16,17). Ananias and his wife Sapphira were removed from this world prematurely because of lying (Acts 5:1-11). Because of sin in the church in Corinth some were "sleeping" in premature graves. If the President had been genuinely converted at seven years of age, as he professed, why is he still alive and living in sin at 51? This should greatly concern the President's ministers.

Christians are morally different because, if they start living like the people of the world, He chastens them. If that fails to work repentance, He takes them out of this world. The only Christians morally equal to the unconverted are in the cemetery.

4. THEY CANNOT
HABITUALLY PRACTICE SIN

Another reason we are not all morally equal is a true

Christian "cannot" practice a life of willful sin. Christians cannot be perfect, but neither can they continue to practice a life of sin. False preachers teach a "carnal security" that is not to be found in the Bible. This is the teaching that says it does not matter if you practice a life of willful sin, you are secure from any retribution. God's grace covers all sin! The Bible warned about this kind of false teachers: "For there are certain men crept in unawares...turning the grace of our God into lasciviousness" (Jude 1:4).

Bill Clinton owes it to himself to read the book *Ten Reasons Why a Christian Does Not Live a Wicked Life* by J. Oliver Buswell, Jr. In it he gives the Biblical proof that anyone continually practicing a life of willful sin is not a Christian. Among the ten reasons are these: First, sin is not the world the Christian lives in: "For one to say, 'I choose to remain in sin because I am saved from its consequences by grace," is a contradiction. When one says, "I am saved, he says by that very fact, "I am not living in the world of sin....Paul says 'We who died to sin, how shall we live any longer in it'" (Romans 6:1,2).[113]

Second, sin is no longer your master: "Paul introduces another figure of speech...'Sin must not reign as King then, in your mortal body, with a view to your obeying his evil desires' (Romans. 6:12)....One who has accepted God's grace has thereby accepted God's gracious Son as his sovereign Lord. One cannot have two kings. Your sovereign is either Christ or sin, not both.[114]...Sin is not going to exercise lordship over you. 'Indeed, you are nor under the wrath and curse of God's law, but you are under the grace of God which is going to reign in your life through justification unto life eternal through Jesus Christ our Lord'" (Romans. 5:21).[115]

Third, sin is no longer the Christian's employer. Buswell points out, "Paul had said, 'Do you not know that if you are working for anyone, you are his employee; you are going to draw wages from him?'...What then? Shall we keep on sinning because we are not under [the curse of] law but under [the reign of] grace? Let it not be! Do you not know that to whom you keep on yielding yourselves as servants for obedience, servants you are to him to whom you give obedience; whether it be servants of sin, [leading] into death, or servants of obedience [to God, leading] into justification?'" (Romans 6:15, 16).[116]

Buswell gives this illustration: "A man is dressed in a Standard Oil uniform. Standard Oil is printed on his cap. Standard Oil is embroidered on his shirt. But this man in the Standard Oil uniform goes to the Shell pump and fills your tank with gas there from. He checks your oil and puts in a quart labeled Shell. He checks the water, cleans the wind-shield, takes your money and places it in the cash register in the Shell office....you say to yourself, 'He must be a Shell employee.'...He may have traded caps and borrowed his buddy's shirt, but he certainly is working for the Shell Company. It is a logical conclusion that at the end of the week he will draw his check as being on the Shell Company's pay-roll....to say, "I choose to live a life of sin because I am 'not under law but under grace' is for him to say, 'I choose to work for the Sin Company. I choose to be under law to draw the wages of sin.'"[117]

Christ died so we would die to sin and live righteous lives: "Who his own self bare our sins in His own body on the tree, that we, being dead to sins, should live unto righteousness" (I Peter 2:24).

THE BIBLICAL BOOK THAT NAILS
THE ERROR OF MORAL EQUIVALENCE

The doctrine of moral equivalence espoused by the

Clinton Clergy runs into its biggest trouble in the book of I John. Here Scripture says a converted person lives a righteous life: "If ye know that he is righteous, ye know that every one that doeth righteousness is born of him" (I John 2:29). I John declares every man that has the hope of heaven in him cleans up his life: "every man that hath this hope in him purifieth himself, even as he is pure" (I John 3:3). This book says a person who has spent years practicing sexual sins has never know God: "Whosoever abideth in him sinneth (does not continue to practice sin) not: whosoever sinneth hath not seen him, neither known him" (I John 3:6). *Matthew Henry's Bible Commentary* explains, "The regenerate person is happily disabled for sin...those who persist in a sinful life sufficiently demonstrate that they are not born of God."

III John reiterates, "Beloved, follow not that which is evil, but that which is good. He that doeth good is of God: but he that doeth evil hath not seen God" (III John 1:11). In his book, *God's Calendar*, Dr. W. O. Vaught said, "as long as one persists in an unrepentant condition, he is out of fellowship with God."[118] But the Bible says a man who persists in an unrepentant condition has never seen God.

The next verse says beware because a lot of people will try to deceive us about this truth: "Little children, let no man deceive you: he that doeth righteousness is righteous, even as he is righteous" (I John 3:7). This is exactly what the Clinton Clergy is trying to do, deceive people into thinking, that they can live in sin just like everyone else and be Christians.

Jesus Christ came into this world to destroy the wicked work of the Devil and enable people to break the bondage of sin: "He that committeth sin is of the devil; for the devil sinneth from the beginning. For this purpose the Son of God was manifested, that he might destroy the works of the devil" (I John 3:8).

The Christian cannot practice a sinful life: "Whosoever is born of God doth not commit sin; for his seed remaineth in him: and he cannot sin, because he is born of God" (I John 3:9). Some preachers want to twist their way out of this hard-hitting truth by changing it to say, "That which is born of God does not commit sin." They say this means the part of you that is saved—your soul—doesn't sin, while the flesh goes right ahead in wickedness. But this isn't what the Bible says. It declares whosoever"—the total person—does not persist in sin.

This is how to tell which people are Christians and which ones are not: "In this the children of God are manifest, and the children of the devil: whosoever doeth not righteousness is not of God, neither he that loveth not his brother" (I John 3:10). They are "manifest" or made plain for all to see. The children of the Devil practice a sinful life. The children of God practice a righteous life.

God is in the business of developing winners over the wickedness of this world: "For whatsoever is born of God overcometh the world: and this is the victory that overcometh the world, even our faith. Who is he that overcometh the world, but he that believeth that Jesus is the Son of God" (I John 5:4,5) He lives in the hearts of true believers to overcome the lust of this world.

The Bible declares God protects His children from the wicked tempter—Satan: "We know that whosoever is born of God sinneth not; but he that is begotten of God keepeth himself, and that wicked one toucheth him not" (I John 5:18).

When the President's Prophets proclaim "we are all sinners" in an attempt to make all men morally equal and hush criticism of the President, they are trashing a central Bible truth. There are two distinctively different classes of people:

the children of light who have been delivered out of their sins and the children of darkness who are still in the bondage of lusts: "Ye are all the children of light, and the children of the day: we are not of the night, nor of darkness" (I Thessalonians 5:5).

All men have been wretched, wicked sinners, but they do not have to stay in that condition. By God's power and grace they can be set free. Jesus can give a fantastic victory. It is regrettable that the Clinton Clergy have not made this clear to the President. Bill Clinton could be a different man today if those responsible for his soul had not instilled in his mind that all are morally equal and nothing can ever change this.

Chapter Nine

THE HIGHCHAIR KING

Clinton's Washington pastor, Rev. J. Philip Wogaman, told his congregation that the Bible is to be seen "as containing truth, like *The New York Times* or *The Washington Post*, but like those newspapers, having errors."[119] Wogaman's "cafeteria Christianity" has contributed to the President's downfall in three ways. First, it has taught him that the Bible is not a reliable moral authority. Second, Wogaman has told Clinton that the human brain is the highest authority and is capable of deciding which parts of the Bible are true and which are error. Third, this communicates to the President that he can write his own commandments about right and wrong. Such beliefs have led the President to think it is right for him to lie and fornicate when he wants to. These things have proved to be Mr. Clinton's moral undoing.

One would expect such anti-Biblical ideas from an out-and-out atheist. But for a man who represents himself as a

Christian minister, this is astonishing. Imagine a man whose only justification for being a preacher is found in the Bible, declaring the Bible contains a bunch of falsehoods. Worse still, the minister accepts a salary from people whose only reason for giving is that the Bible tells them to. Then he turns around and tells them the Bible is not true. At least the proverbial dog just bites the hand that feeds him. He doesn't run all over the country telling everybody the man who fed him is a liar and wreck his reputation. But this is what Rev. Wogaman does to the Book that provides him his bread.

How does the Founders United Methodist minister justify all this? How does he go on saying, "The Bible bears witness to that gospel; it is not the gospel itself." The gospel, it appears, is what Wogaman says it to be, not what the Bible says it is.

CLINTON WAS TAUGHT HE DOESN'T HAVE TO ACCEPT BIBLE'S AUTHORITY

Clinton's pastor leaves no room for misunderstanding. He says, "Anyone who reads the Bible, the whole Bible, very carefully will discover contradictions, different versions of the same event, claims made that stretch our credulity to the breaking point, even a questionable moral teaching and radically different portraits of God. Is It possible to hold all that together in a serious way, really believing that it is all so?"[120]

The President's Washington pastor expresses concern about people who have been "injured" by "literalistic interpretations of scriptural passages." He told his congregation: "There are inconsistencies in the Bible....There are parts of the Bible no longer consistent with deep convictions of faith and moral life that we now share." He even drew laughter from his congregation by ridiculing the Scripture condemning homosexuality and renounced the virgin birth of Jesus!

Wogaman advocates not taking the Bible "literally" but taking it "seriously:" "There are quite a few Christians who would answer quite simply: to take the Bible seriously is to believe it. 'God said it. I believe it. That settles it.'...About two centuries ago, biblical scholars began a more careful examination of Scripture, applying to the Bible the kind of analysis that might be used with other forms of literature.[121] This investigation leads to the learned conclusion that we cannot take the Bible literally, but seriously," according to Wogaman.

Here is where Rev. Wogaman gets into trouble. With unparalleled confidence the Bible claims for itself inspiration by God. II Timothy 3:16 says, "All Scripture is given by inspiration of God." II Peter 1:21 says, "For the prophecy came not in old times by the will of man; but holy men of God spake as they were moved by the Holy Ghost." Two thousand times the Old Testament prophets claim they are quoting God. Daniel said, "When I heard the voice of his words" (Daniel 10:9). Hosea said, "The word of the Lord that came unto Hosea," (Hosea 1:1). Joel 1:1 says, "The word of the Lord that came to Joel." Amos said, "Hear the word of the Lord" (3:1). Obadiah said, "Thus saith the Lord God" (1:1). Habakkuk wrote, "The Lord answered me and said" (2:2). Sixty times Ezekiel said, "His writings were the words of God." Nothing in the Bible is made clearer than the claim that the "words" of the Bible are dictated by God.

Clinton's Washington pastor cannot believe Jesus without believing the Bible is God's infallible writing. Luke 24:27 says, "And beginning at Moses and all the prophets, he (Jesus) expounded unto them in all the Scriptures the things concerning himself." In Luke 24:44 Jesus said, "These are the words which I spake unto you, while I was yet with you, that all things must be fulfilled, which were written in the law of

Moses, and in the prophets, and in the psalms, concerning me. Here Jesus took the three divisions of the Old Testament and declared them all authentic. In Matthew 5:18 Jesus said, "For verily I say unto you, Till heaven and earth pass, one jot or one tittle shall in no wise pass from the law, till all be fulfilled." A tittle is less that the cross on a T; a jot is a half-sized letter. Then Jesus took the two hardest things in the Bible for people like the Clinton Clergy to believe—the flood, in Luke 17:27, and the fish swallowing Jonah, in Matthew 12:40—and put his stamp of truth upon them.

If the Bible is not all literally true, then Wogaman is completely justified when he refuses to accept the Biblical injunctions against homosexuality and its declaration of Jesus' virgin birth. It also means President Clinton is completely justified if he refuses to accept the Biblical injunctions against lying and lust. He can simply say, "The learned Reverend says it is not all accurate. I believe these particular Scriptures are inaccurate." Wogaman puts it to us straight. Either we must believe his writings or the Bible. One of the two books has to be in error.

WISE MEN HAVE APPLAUDED
THE BIBLE AS AUTHORITATIVE

Wiser men than Wogaman have seen the Bible in a more positive light than the Clinton Clergy. Abraham Lincoln said of the Bible, "This book is the best gift God has given to man, but for it we could not know right from wrong. Read this book for what own reason you can except and take the rest on faith and you will live and die a better man." Ulysses S. Grant said, "Hold fast to the Bible at the sheet anchor of your liberties, write its precepts in your heart, practice them in your lives to the influence of the book we are indebted for all of the progress made in true civilization and to this we must look as our guide in the future. Righteousness exalteth a nation but sin is a reproach to any people."

George Wald, a Professor of Biology at Harvard, received tremendous applause from the scholars gathered at Southern Colorado State College when he said, "The only way the world is going to stop short of the brink of nuclear holocaust is a return to God and the principles of the Bible. The greatest question facing civilization today is, 'Is the Bible a revelation of the God who created the universe showing us the way out of our dilemma or is the Bible only an archaic book of folk stories written by men?'"

PRESIDENT IS TAUGHT THE HIGHEST AUTHORITY IN THE UNIVERSE IS RIGHT BEHIND HIS EYEBALLS

Rev. Wogaman says, "One does not have to be a biblical literalist, accepting every part of the Bible...to acknowledge the foundational nature of Scripture....one feels compelled to say that the Bible also contains material that, if pursued mechanically, would take you *away* from the gospel."[122] Strange, the book that brought the gospel to the world is accused of leading people away from the gospel. Not content to merely accuse the Bible of containing non-truths, Wogaman must attack it. And by what authority does he reject it? His brain! In his mind, some Scripture is inaccurate and other Scripture actually takes us away from the gospel. Therefore, we must appeal to a higher authority than the Bible. We must rely on our brain to tell us what is right and what is wrong.

This sends President Clinton the clear message that what his mind tells him he should do is right and if his Bible contradicts this, the Bible is wrong. He must not only refuse to submit to the authority of the Bible, he must obey the higher authority, his mind.

ANY MAN CAN WRITE HIS OWN
SET OF COMMANDMENTS

Wogaman goes so far as to say it is "tempting" to accept the Bible as our moral authority: "The most tempting source of authority is the Bible....When a specific passage supports a point we wish to make, we may simply use the passage as authority...But if we rely upon a particular proof text in this way, we are unconsciously committed to accept every other Biblical passage on every other issue. I have known both 'conservative' and 'liberal' preaching to fall into this trap."[123] Rev. Wogaman declares that when we accept a text in the Bible as literally true, we are falling into a trap. Obviously, this is not a trap Wogaman has fallen into.

Wogaman proceeds to write his own list of commands. This minister who refuses to accept God's commandments has no trouble laying down his own dogmatic moral absolutes. Here are the commandments according to Wogaman:

I. "Thou shalt not practice capitalism." In 1990 he declared that unrestrained capitalism was the cause of drug abuse, divorce, murder and unethical business practices. Economic inequality is unacceptable, he said.

II. "Thou shalt not interfere with abortions." In his book, *Protestant Faith and Religious Liberty*, Clinton's preacher commended the 1973 Supreme Court legalization of abortion as "a landmark of humane spirit and practical wisdom," and said having an abortion "may be faithful obedience to the God of life and love." He told *The Washington Post* that a ban on late-term abortion would be 'unfeeling.'

III. "Thou shalt not pollute the environment." Under a heading "Naming the Evils" Wogaman writes this commandment. He uses the illustration of a child dying because a community neglected its drinking water. He declared this was a "sin."

IV. "Thou shalt not disapprove of homosexuals." His church is one of only 87 United Methodist churches out of the denomination's 37,000 that have signed up for a program to reconcile homosexuals and rejected Methodism's historic disapproval of their practices.

V. "Thou shalt love Communism." Wogaman informed us, during the Cold War, that "The USSR is characteristic of the more tolerant Communist arrangements for religion...It is highly questionable whether Christians in Russia or China are treated any worse than Marxists in the United States."

VI. "Thou shalt embrace world government." According to the Rev., "Global government" may be the only solution to the planet's conflicts.

Mark Tooley says Wogaman "exemplifies the new, postmodern clergyman, obsessed with political issues, theologically casual, and employing his church as a bully pulpit for politically correct social ideas." This is the kind of clergyman who produces the Bill Clinton kind of disciple—men trying to control society who cannot control their own bodies.

Following the example of his minister, Clinton has every right to step up and write the Clinton Commandments. These dictates could include:

I. "Thou shalt not deny your body anything it desires, for this is against nature."

II. "Thou shalt not lose the power of the presidency, whatever the price."

III. "Thou shalt lie when it is necessary to achieve noble goals.

IV. Thou shalt viciously attack your accusers and destroy them when you can. Such is the just reward of these enemies."

V. "Thou shalt not be concerned about friends. It is every man for himself. Do not worry when they run up huge legal bills because of your misconduct."

PROPPING UP A HIGHCHAIR KING

When a man has climbed to the highest seat the world has to offer, the American presidency, where does he go? The only higher position is the throne of the King. Never mind that the Bible says, "Thou shalt have no other God before me" (Exodus 20:3). Wogaman says you can't believe all that stuff anyway. Besides, one writer has already crowned Bill Clinton a king. Maureen Dowd says, "In psychology, they have a term for a narcissist who never emotionally matures, who throws tantrums and expects everyone else to clean up his messes: the Highchair King....Bill Clinton's most authentic moment was his Monica speech. He was unbound, unvarnished and true to himself. He resented apologizing for his bad behavior. He did it sullenly, only because all escape hatches were closed. He was still trying to blame others and still expecting others to prop him up—especially the strong women in his life."[124]

Bill Clinton followed the beliefs of Rev. Philip Wogaman and they have led him to the throne—the throne of a buffoon, the throne of late-night comedy jokes. Such destruction of a human being is something to weep about. Wogaman wrote his own little Bible he calls *Speaking the Truth in Love*. However, if Wogaman had any love for anything other than his own position, if he had any love for President Clinton and the other souls in his congregation, he would stop preaching lies about the Bible and start preaching the eternal truth of God's Word. At least Bill Clinton was man enough to finally admit he misled the American people. Is it too much to hope that his clergyman do the same?

Chapter Ten

THE PRESIDENT, THE PILOT
AND THE PREACHER

Speaking on *Larry King Live*, Bishop J. T. Jakes says that job performance is more important than character or conduct. Jakes offered this analogy of the Clinton crisis: "I think they (the American people) are somewhat in a dilemma as it relates to the performance of the president. Flying in to be here in California, I was on a 747 jet. I would like to think that the pilot who flew the flight in was a moral person and had good integrity and was faithful to his wife. But 38, 000 feet in the air I am more concerned that he is able to function and do his job."[125] Jakes separates character from job performance and chooses job performance as the more important issue. Bishop Jakes must have made a misstatement. It is hard to believe a minister would confess that his safety is more important than a pilot's soul.

The author of the bestselling book, *The Lady, Her*

Lover and Her Lord, is a welcome addition to the Clinton Clergy. Jakes provides the President with an articulate man of the cloth spinning the White House spin that Clinton is doing a good job, which is the most important thing. To do this requires Jakes to minimize sin, making job performance the main issue.

Jakes' book is a run-away best-seller, but his *The President, The Pilot and The Preacher* is something quite different.

PRESIDENT TOLD JOB PERFORMANCE AND MORALS ARE SEPARATE THINGS

Would Jakes be content if his pilot was fornicating with a company flight attendant in the work place, while maneuvering his plane and talking to the control tower? This type of situation is exactly what the President has been charged with arranging. Monica Lewinsky, a government employee, says she and the President had sexual relations in the White House, reportedly while foreign dignitaries waited outside. And on another occasion, it is said to have occurred while the President was on the phone with a staff member. I am sure if Bishop Jakes thought it through, he would prefer his to pilot to avoid such distraction while flying his airplane. Passion distracts a person from focusing on the work at hand. It would not matter if he was the most capable pilot on earth. Most of us would prefer the pilot to keep his mind and body devoted to flying the plane.

Jakes picked an interesting analogy to use in his apparent defense of the President. I asked a airline pilot what would happen if he was caught having sex with a company employee in the workplace. He quickly replied, "I'd be gone instantly. The company has a very strict policy about this." No airline in America would hesitate to fire a pilot who did this. The redemption Rev. Jakes stresses would be secondary. Passenger safety would come first. The airline would take the pilot off the job immediately. Perhaps they would secure help for him later. There might even come a day when he would be allowed to fly again. But, in the short term, he is out. So, to press Rev. Jakes' analogy demands the immediate dismissal of Mr. Clinton from the Presidency.

CLINTON TOLD MORALS
DO NOT AFFECT JOB PERFORMANCE

Rev. Jakes might not think character is as important as skill. But when a pilot announces, "Welcome aboard Fight 889 to Atlanta," most people like to think their pilot is telling them the truth. If the pilot is a liar, this can be a problem. He might just be saying he is flying to the Georgia hub when he is actually diverting the plane to Cuba. When the pilot announces "There is going to be a ten-minute delay in our departure," most passengers expect this to be the truth. If the pilot doesn't know, if there is a possibility the flight will be canceled, most passengers would like be told. The truth would enable them to check the travel schedule for a backup flight. It would mean they could call the people meeting them at their destination and tell them, "Don't head for the airport. Check with the airline. I do not know when I will arrive."

Honesty is important. The Commandment "thou shalt not bear false witness" counts big with most airline passengers.

MINISTER SAYS, COMMIT ADULTERY
AND BE A BETTER CHRISTIAN

Jakes is not the only one minimizing sin. "When leaders are going through storms, their ministers and their faith fortify," said the Rev. Jesse Jackson. The minister Clinton leaned on after the Lewinsky controversy broke says the storm over President Clinton's adulterous affair will fortify his faith. As your faith is fortified, you become a better Christian. Therefore, in the gospel according to Rev. Jackson, the storm over his exposed adultery will make Clinton a better Christian.

"We know that the dark clouds will be rolled away if you are faithful and focused and disciplined," continues Rev. Jackson. He chooses beautiful words that have a great breadth of interpretation: "Faithful" to the work of the presidency, or "faithful" to Jehovah God? "Focused" on being head of government or "focused" on repentance of sin? "Disciplined" to carry on the daily tasks in the White House or "disciplined" to control the fiery sexual passion raging within his heart?

But Clinton's Washington pastor can even top Rev. Jackson. He says Clinton's sinning could be a blessing. "True, the report (of Clinton's sexual misconduct) was pornographic," Rev. Philip Wogaman said. But it "could even be viewed as a blessing, because it forced him to face up to things. And he committed himself to the hard work of repentance." Isn't this great. Rev. Wogaman has learned the secret of bringing sinners to repentance. Just publish their secret sins and watch them flock to the altar. This discovery should enable him to convert nearly everybody in Washington. When Wogaman says Starr's report forced the President to face up to things and repent, he is blindly ignoring the fact that it has not forced him to face up to his critical castigation of Kenneth Starr. Neither has it led him to repent of driving his staff toward bankruptcy with legal bills incurred because of the President's lie. This would require reimbursement.

Rev. Jakes misses a main point in his analogy. A pilots works in relative privacy. He sits in the isolation of his cockpit, speaks few words and is rarely seen. But the President is seen on TV nearly every day. His words echo around the world by radio. Newspapers report his every move. He is the most influential person in the world. To compare a pilot with a president shows a reckless disregard for the important of influence.

But despite the pilot's minimal influence on his passengers, his company is extremely concerned with the influence he does have. They want him smiling, greeting passengers when he has time, dressing appropriately and refraining from any hint of immoral conversation or action in front of the passengers. A pilot who told a dirty joke to a flight attendant within earshot of a 10-year-old passenger would be reprimanded very severely. Image and influence are essential to the airlines.

THE GRAVE CRIME OF MINIMIZING SIN

It would be an error for any Clinton spin doctor to use Rev. Jakes' airline analogy. But when Jakes minimizes sin, with this airline theology, he is failing in his duty to the President. Jakes does a great job of emphasizing the grace of God and restoration of sinners, but when he stepped over into the political arena, he sent out a message that appears to make light of the evils he fights. This does Mr. Clinton no good.

Speaking on the *Larry King Live* program with Jakes, former Marine Chuck Colson said, "I would use another analogy....If you are in combat, you care a whole lot more about the fellow in the next fox hole, not about his IQ, whether it is 150 or 160, but whether he is a man of honor that will keep his word that you can trust and that you can depend on. I think what the American people are beginning to understand is that character does count."[126]

To under state the horrors of sin is to under state the very things that have brought Mr. Clinton so much misery. Psalm 38:3 says, "There is no soundness in my flesh...neither is there any rest in my bones because of my sin." Lady Macbeth spoke for Bill Clinton and a thousand tortured souls when she loosed this conscience-scourged cry, "Out, out damned spot... all the perfumes of Arabia could not sweeten this little hand"? King David said, "There is no soundness in my flesh because of thine anger; neither is there any rest in my bones because of my sin. For mine iniquities are gone over mine head: as an heavy burden they are too heavy for me" (Psalm 38:3-4). The prophet Isaiah declared, "the wicked are like the troubled sea, when it cannot rest, whose waters cast up mire and dirt" (Isaiah 57:20). Sin can only be minimized by those who do not care for the misery it causes its victims.

To downplay sin is to downplay the thing that has reduced Mr. Clinton to a slave of lust. In John 8:34 Jesus says, "Whosoever committeth sin is the servant of sin." "His own iniquities shall take the wicked himself, and he shall be holden with the cords of his sins" (Proverbs 5:22). In 1981, when Bill Clinton was out of the governor's office, he gave a guest lecture at the University of Arkansas in Fayetteville. Clinton told the class about the unending struggle between darkness and light and how it related to family disorders, insecurity and depression.[127] Tragically, Mr. Clinton has had to struggle thoughout his life with the sins that have progressively enslaved him.

To underestimate the terrors of sin is to underestimate the great enemy of Bill Clinton's family: "The LORD is longsuffering, and of great mercy, forgiving iniquity and transgression, and by no means clearing the guilty, visiting the iniquity of the fathers upon the children unto the third and fourth generation" (Numbers 14:18). Children pay when fathers sin. Can't you imagine the President's wife and daughter saying, "Honey don't worry about having sex with the girls, you are doing a great job of running the country, that is all that matters."

When President Bill Clinton was sworn in on January 20, 1993, he had his hand on a Bible. It was opened to Galatians 6:7,8. The passage says, "Be not deceived; God is not mocked: for whatsoever a man soweth, that shall he also reap. For he that soweth to his flesh shall of the flesh reap corruption; but he that soweth to the Spirit shall of the Spirit reap life everlasting." Today, reaping a harvest of corruption because of his misconduct, he has become the classic illustration of this warning about sin.

To reduce the importance of sin is to reduce the importance of the exposer of Clinton's shame. Sin is a betrayer which "will out" no matter what pains are taken to hide it: "Your transgressions are discovered, so that in all your doings your sins do appear" (Ezekiel 21:24). Kenneth Starr is not the exposer. He is only the tool. Sin is the real betrayer. *The New York Times* said, "Here was a man of compassionate impulse and lofty ambition who went to Washington with virtually every imaginable political skill except one. He seemed to think he was immune from a rule that leaps out from any reading of modern presidencies. Everything comes out sooner or later."[128]

To lower sins importance is to lower the importance of a sickness which contaminates Bill Clinton's entire being: "Ah sinful nation, a people laden with iniquity, a seed of evildoers, children that are corrupters: they have forsaken the LORD...the whole head is sick, and the whole heart faint" (Isaiah 1:4, 5). *The Anchorage Times* wrote, "Clinton has thrown himself into the trash heap of history. And the nation has reason to mourn the shame he has brought to his office"[129] No cancer could be more devastating to the life of Mr. Clinton than the sickness his sin has brought.

To minimize sin is to minimize the thing that has become a reproach to our nation. Proverbs 14:34 says,

"Righteousness exalteth a nation: but sin is a reproach to any people." Dr. Laura Schlessinger, a Jewish lady who hosts a radio talk show, speaks with a boldness rarely found in today's world. The host—known as "Dr. Laura"—has risen to number one by filling a void for the many people who do not have a strong moral voice in their pulpit. She says, "They've become a bunch of camp counselors instead of moral leaders. They follow instead of leading. They are pop psychologists who tell people it is all right to do whatever they feel like doing."[130]

Dr. Laura, the author of *The Ten Commandments: the Significance of God's Laws in Everyday Life*, does not bite her tongue about the Clinton fall: "He probably started out by breaking the 10th one (Commandments)—Thou shalt not covet'—needing more power or whatever he needed from a 21-year-old...Then he moved on to the seventh—adultery— and the ninth, when he lied."[131]

Dale Hanson Bourke, says, "What really ticks her (Dr. Laura) off is her belief Clinton also dissed the third command- ment—that many call the 'swearing commandment,' the one about taking God's name in vain. Schlessinger believes that commandment is violated any time we shame our God, espe- cially when we have a position of authority."[132] This is pointed preaching on sin that properly attacks it.

AN OPPORTUNITY LOST

The Presidential Prophets have failed in a unique opportunity to "Cry aloud, spare not, lift up thy voice like a trumpet, and shew my people their transgression" (Isaiah 58:1).

Tragically, this minimizing of sin is not confined just to the Clinton Clergy. Jerry Falwell, speaking on the same *Larry King Live* program as Jakes, pointed out, "There are 600,000 pastors in America. If you ask me where is the major responsibility for America's moral free fall, I would have to put it on the door steps of our churches. Because there has been a deafening silence (regarding sin) in America's pulpits."

The Washington Times editor, Wes Pruden, says: "Dwight Moody and Billy Sunday, earlier giants of evangelism, never cut public sin any slack. The silence of preacher (today) with the duty to denounce sin is deafening and is the meaningless chatter of holy men with nothing to say to a 'faithless and perverse generation.' This leaves the field clear for shameless and secular men to mug facts and maim truth, seducing an ever widening pool of patsies."[133]

President Clinton, fighting to hold off impeachment on December 11, 1998, quoted *The Rubaiyat*, the classic poem by Omar Khayyam,

"The moving finger writes;
      And having writ moves on. Nor all you piety nor wit
Shall lure it back to cancel half a line,
      Nor all your tears wash out a word of it."

The President said he understands that to mean neither tears, nor torment, "can alter what I have done." The "moving finger" Khayyam referred to is in the Book of Daniel, "In the same hour came forth fingers of a man's hand, and wrote over against the candlestick upon the plaster of the wall of the king's palace...God hath numbered thy kingdom, and finished it...Thou art weighed in the balances, and art found wanting" (Daniel 5:5,26,27). That night King Belshazzar's reign over Babylon ended as the Persians conquered the land. The handwriting on the wall was final. the King was finished.

Cal Thomas, in a column on December 15, 1998, regarding the President's quote, said, "the poem cited by President Clinton as worthy of his and our consideration contains a deeper and far more important message for him. He also (like King Belshazzar), has demonstrated arrogance and pride...As Omar Khayyam put it in what could be another strong message for the President should he wish to read further:

'Indeed the Idols I have loved so long
    'Have done my credit in this World much wrong;
'Have drowned my Glory in a shallow Cup,
    'And sold my Reputation for a Song.'"[187]

    Silence about sin produces victims of sin, like King Belshazzar and President Clinton.

Chapter Eleven

HOW THE PRESIDENT'S CHURCH FAILED HIM

When the president of Southern Seminary, Southern Baptist's largest theological seminary, called on President Clinton's home church to enforce Biblical discipline on him, the church would not even discuss it. Dr. R. Albert Mohler, Jr. said, "How can President Clinton claim to be a Southern Baptist and persist in this public display of serial sin?" In a August 24, 1998 column, Mohler explained, "Only because the congregation which holds his membership has failed to exercise any semblance of church discipline. Southern Baptists will be watching the Immanuel Baptist Church in Little Rock to see if it musters the courage to make clear its own convictions."[134]

Even this mention of Biblical discipline stirred a firestorm. Upon reading Mohler's appeal for action, columnist Gracie Bonds Staples declared, "My heart sank... Mohler's ...holier-than-thou attitude has stayed with me because I think it is so contrary to everything Christianity is." Staples cannot conceive of forgiveness and church discipline being compatible, "As a child of the 'born again,' one of the earliest lessons I learned was how I ought to pray and ask God to 'forgive us our trespasses as we forgive those who trespass against us."[186]

CLINTON'S CLERGYMEN DENIED THERE WAS A NEED FOR DISCIPLINE

When Clinton's Arkansas pastor, Rev. Rex Horne, was contacted by reporters about Mohler's statement, he declined to speak with them. Instead, he issued this statement which totally ignored any responsibility for carrying out the Bible's commands regarding discipline: "The recent admission of immoral conduct by the President is grievous. His actions are indefensible and inexcusable. They are not, however unforgivable. I pray the President will find the grace of God, which comes upon confession of sin and the peace which comes from a restored relationship with our Lord."[135]

After the cries for discipline by the church, President Clinton sent a handwritten letter to his home church in Arkansas in which he requested the church's forgiveness. Horne said the President "expressed repentance for his actions, sadness for the consequence of his sin on his family, friends and church family and asked for forgiveness from Immanuel."[136] The pastor refuses to enter into the debate over disciplining Clinton. He merely says as a pastor he has "a responsibility to do what's right before the Lord and for our church."

Rev. Horne is correct about the President's sins being forgivable. They are. Praying for the President is appropriate. But Horne and the Immanuel Baptist Church have a God-given responsibility to follow a clearly outlined plan for restoring members who have strayed. They have chosen to disobey this Biblical outline regarding a straying member. As long as Bill Clinton's church refuses to follow the Bible's clear instructions, they share in the guilt of every sin Bill Clinton commits.

THE SOUTHERN BAPTIST DENOMINATION'S POSITION

Adriana Soloun, of Hanford California, wrote a letter to the editor of *USA Weekend*, asking, "Our repentant president often is photographed going to church. What is his church, and does it require any public penance or discipline?" The editor replied, "President Clinton is a Southern Baptist; discipline is up to individual churches. Clinton's home church, Immanuel Baptist in Little Rock, has taken no steps to discipline him, but last month he wrote to his pastor expressing sorrow and seeking forgiveness. In Washington, the Clintons attend Foundry United Methodist (Hillary's affiliation), which has no public discipline process."[137]

William Merrell, a spokesman for the Southern Baptist Executive Committee, said, "We do get a pretty large number of calls here—some of them quite irate—that the Southern Baptist Convention has not taken steps to discipline or to otherwise exhort Mr. Clinton....We (the Executive Committee) do not have the authority or the capacity nor do we desire either of those to define a church's membership or its membership policies."

Merrell stressed that our Baptist forebearers were persecuted by centralized church movements, and have a tradition of strongly supporting congregational independence. An attempt to have the Southern Baptist Convention call for Immanuel Baptist Church to discipline President Clinton because of his support for homosexuals was voted down. At the June, 1998 convention a resolution was passed calling on

Congress to nullify a presidential directive barring discrimination in the federal workplace on the basis of sexual orientation. But an attempt to amend the resolution with a call for the President's church to discipline him for his actions was narrowly defeated. "I don't think it failed because the people didn't believe Mr. Clinton needs to take very seriously the spiritual jeopardy in which a Christian places himself when he adopts a sub-Christian, anti-Christian lifestyle, but rather because there's a very good sense among Baptists of what is appropriate," said Merrell.[138]

Mr. Merrell correctly stresses the Baptist tradition of strongly supporting congregational independence. He does not stress that Baptists also have a strong tradition of believing the Bible and that the Bible clearly commands discipline of straying members. When Merrell says, "there's a very good sense among Baptists of what is appropriate," he appears to be shifting the guidelines of authority from what is Biblical to what is appropriate. Certainly, ignoring disciplining means the church does not bring down the wrath of the media on the Immanuel Baptist Church, anger any other members practicing a sinful life style, or hurt the income of the church. If by "appropriate," Mr. Merrell means "what is good business," Immanuel Baptist Church is doing the appropriate thing.

On the other hand, if by "appropriate" Mr. Merrell means "what is Biblical," if it means lovingly confronting the President, working to lead him out of his sins and removing his name from the church role if he refused to change, then the action is not at all appropriate.

Certainly, neither Mr. Merrell nor the Convention has any explicit Biblical responsibility to chastise Mr. Clinton. The church does. The Christians in Immanuel Baptist Church would do well to heed the admonition of Dr. R. Albert Mohler, Jr., and take the action the Bible demands. Christians across the nation would do well to join Mohler's cry for Biblical discipline. If a person believes the Bible to be the authoritative Word of God, he or she has to believe that the Lord has given us the best way to help fallen members.

On August 27, 1998, a dozen religious leaders signed "A Pastoral Letter to the Nation" calling for the nation to put the matter of Clinton's immorality behind them without mention of Biblical discipline: "It is time to put to rest what has occurred, to do things that will set this matter right and to focus anew on the news in our own land and threats to stability, justice and peace in our world." Among those signing this letter were the Rev. Joan Brown Campbell, general secretary of the National Council of Churches; the Rev. Gardner Taylor, pastor emeritus, Concord Baptist Church in Brooklyn, N.Y.; and Rabbi Arthur Schneier, senior rabbi of Park East Synagogue.[139]

These clergymen call for the nation to focus on "threats to stability, justice and peace." It seems strange that they do not call for the country to focus on God, the Bible, and repentance, as clergymen would be expected to do. It is also strange that they call for the people to "do things that will set this matter right" with no reference to what the Bible says will set it right. Apparently, these men have departed from their only justification for being clergymen, the Bible, and have replaced it with a new supreme authority of their personal opinion.

THE EFFECTS OF HIS CHURCH'S NEGLECT ON THE PRESIDENT

Refusing discipline is the most unkind thing the Immanuel Baptist Church can do to Bill Clinton. When a school refuses to discipline an unruly student it increases the chances that student will never reach his potential in life. When a ball team refuses to discipline its loafing members, it increases the chances that the team will lose its games. When a therapist neglects to discipline a patient to endure the pain and increase his muscular movement, he or she increases the chances the patient will not fully recover. When an army refuses to discipline an erring soldier, it increases the chances the soldier will lose his life and the army will lose the battle. When churches neglect the discipline of straying members, they increase the chances the straying will continue, lives will be ruined and souls will be lost. When preachers refuse to discipline erring members, they do those members a most unkind service.

Our family has had first-hand experience with church discipline. An uncle became involved with a woman who was not his wife. He ended up leaving his wife and marrying her. The Baptist church of which he had been a member, voted to remove him from the membership roll. It was a painful ordeal for everyone. However, there was never even a rumor that he ever had another affair.

Had Immanuel Baptist Church practiced the Bible's plan for helping a fallen member early on, back when Clinton was defeated for governor, humbled and attending church actively, there is a good chance his straying might have been corrected. This would have meant the entire tragedy could have been averted. The church failed to do this.

CHRIST'S 4-STEP PROGRAM FOR DEALING WITH CHURCH MEMBERS LIVING IN SIN

God has given a carefully written prescription for helping people in Mr. Clinton's shape. It is a four-step redemptive program designed to awaken a church member who is practicing a life of sin: Jesus said "Moreover if thy brother shall trespass against thee, go and tell him his fault between thee and him alone: if he shall hear thee, thou hast gained thy brother. But if he will not hear thee, then take with thee one or two more, that in the mouth of two or three witnesses every word may be established. And if he shall neglect to hear them, tell it unto the church: but if he neglect to hear the church, let him be unto thee as an heathen man and a publican" (Matthew 18:15-17).

1. GO TO THE ERRING MEMBER PRIVATELY

First, we are instructed to go to the fellow member alone and tell him his fault. When the first stories of Mr. Clinton's involvement with women surfaced, the church should have moved into action. Some member with information about this conduct should have confronted him with the charges. That member should have prayed with him and rebuked him. II Timothy 4:2 says, "reprove, rebuke, exhort with all longsuffering and doctrine." If that member hears and repents, a brother's restoration has been gained.

2. CARRY A GROUP TO HIM AND TRY AGAIN

Second, if our first effort fails, we are to take one or two of our fellow church members with us and try again. In this case, we should tell the member that the matter will be brought up publicly before the church if he does not repent. If this fails, we have at least established the facts with other witnesses.

3. BRING HIM BEFORE THE CHURCH

Third, if all private attempts have failed, we must now tell the church. There are to be no cover-ups. The church should then urge the member to repent of his sins. The Bible says, "Them that sin rebuke before all, that others also may fear" (I Timothy 5:20). Hopefully, the member will be persuaded to repent when the whole church exhorts him.

Jesus said, "Take heed to yourselves: If thy brother trespass against thee, rebuke him; and if he repent, forgive him" (Luke 17:3). Mr. Clinton's church should have "rebuked" him for his conduct. If a singer sings poorly, the music instructor rebukes him. If a basketball player misses shots, the coach rebukes him. If the soldier shoots wrong, the sergeant rebukes him. And when a Christian lives wrong, his church must rebuke him. This is the way we are to help people doing wrong in any field.

Silence gives approval. If a child starts to put a rock in his mouth or stick his hand in a fire and the parents say nothing, the child assumes the behavior is all right. When a church sees a member practicing a life of adultery yet says nothing, that member has to assume his behavior to be acceptable. The Immanuel Baptist Church stands condemned by its silence—condemned by its refusal to rebuke Bill Clinton.

4. TREAT HIM LIKE AN UNCONVERTED HEATHEN

As a last resort, if our private and public rebukes have failed, we must assume the person to be an unconverted heathen. Jesus said, "If he neglect to hear the church, let him be unto thee as an heathen man" (Matthew 18:17). This means removing him from the church to awake him to the fact he is not a Christian, and praying for his salvation.

The Apostle Paul followed Christ's instruction when dealing with a church member in Corinth who was engaged in a shameful, sexual sin: "It is reported commonly that there is fornication among you, and such fornication as is not so much as named among the Gentiles, that one should have his father's wife. And ye are puffed up, and have not rather mourned, that he that hath done this deed might be taken away from among you. For I verily, as absent in body, but present in spirit, have judged already, as though I were present, concerning him that hath so done this deed, In the name of our Lord Jesus Christ, when ye are gathered together, and my spirit, with the power of our Lord Jesus Christ, To deliver such an one unto Satan for the destruction of the flesh, that the spirit may be saved in the day of the Lord Jesus" (I Corinthians 5:1-5). Paul is practicing what Jesus commanded, "Let him be unto thee as an heathen man and a publican." Obviously, Paul assumes a man refusing to repent of flagrant sin is an unsaved heathen. The purpose of his removal is that his "spirit may be saved." If he were already saved, nothing would need to be done to assure his spirit would be saved. Outside of the church, with sin destroying his flesh, he could be led to salvation, hopefully.

If Mr. Clinton had refused to confess his sin and repent, he should have been informed that he was facing removal from the church. This would have been a formidable threat against a politician in a Christian state. It would have worked to awaken him to his need for repentance. It would also have served to awaken other members to the necessity of living a godly life. And most important, it would preserve the reputation of the church and the honor of the Lord Jesus Christ.

Dr. Adrian Rogers, pastor of the Bellevue Baptist Church in Memphis, Tennessee, and three time president of the Southern Baptist Convention, said, "The reason we vote people into the church is, if you don't vote them in you can't vote them out."

Some Mennonites follow the Bible's restoration plan in every detail. They will not even sit down and eat with someone who is a professing Christian living in flagrant sin. The practice is a church ordinance call "shunning." They even set up a separate table in the house for a prodigal son to use until he repents. This is based on a clear Bible teaching, "I wrote unto you in an epistle not to company with fornicators:

Yet not altogether with the fornicators of this world, or with the covetous, or extortioners, or with idolaters; for then must ye needs go out of the world. But now I have written unto you not to keep company, if any man that is called a brother be a fornicator, or covetous, or an idolater, or a railer, or a drunkard, or an extortioner; with such an one no not to eat" (I Corinthians 5:9-11). The practice of shunning serves as a constant reminder of a person's need to repent and protects the reputation of the other church members.

Matthew Henry's Commentary says, "They were to avoid all familiarity with him; they were to have no commerce with him...that they might shame him, and bring him to repentance, must disclaim and shun him...Christians are to avoid the familiar conversation of fellow-Christians that are notoriously wicked, and under just censure for their...practices. Such disgrace the Christian name."

The dynamic New Testament church enforced such teachings of the apostles upon the members: "As they went through the cities, they delivered them the decrees for to keep, that were ordained of the apostles and elders which were at Jerusalem. And so were the churches established in the faith, and increased in number daily" (Acts 16:4,5). There were authoritarian rules to keep in the New Testament church. The church protected its reputation by exerting this authority over the members. As a result of a fantastic reputation, these churches increased in number daily. The Immanuel Baptist Church would help Bill Clinton, its own reputation, and would contribute to the growth of the church if it would exert its God-given authority to deal with Mr. Clinton's bad conduct. In addition, such action would benefit not only the President and the church, but also many Christians. If the church would speak out against the President's sin, it would teach others to fear such conduct. This would contribute to the moral health of the nation.

THE ASSEMBLIES OF GOD
PROVIDE AN EXAMPLE

The Assemblies of God are an example of a major American denomination that practices the Biblical program of discipline. They removed Jimmy Swaggart ministerial papers when he refused to submit to the church's restoration program. This required a serious commitment to the rules of Scripture because he was contributing a reported $10 million a year to the denomination's mission program. The Assemblies were amazed that after losing that huge sum, the following year they received more for missions. Though Swaggart is preaching today, he is not doing it as an Assemblies of God minister. Here are passages from the manual describing the discipline program:

> **"Discipline Grounds**
> Discipline is an exercise of scriptural authority for which the church is responsible (Matthew 16:19, 18:15-20; Luke 17:3; John 20:23; Acts 16:4; Ephesians 5:11; I Timothy 5:20; II Timothy 4:2; Hebrews 13:17). The purpose of discipline is to promote repentance and restoration through exposing sinful behavior. It is to be redemptive in nature as well as corrective. Any member of the assembly is subject to discipline on the basis of unscriptural conduct or doctrinal departure from the Tenets of Faith of this assembly.
>
> The discipline of pastors is administered by the district Presbytery.

Procedure
The assembly will follow the disciplinary procedure set forth in Matthew 18:15-20. This procedure consists generally of the following steps: (1) The pastor or a designated member of the church board discusses the charges with the member in an effort to resolve the matter privately; (2) if the first step does not resolve the matter, then the member shall meet with the pastor and church board or with designated committee of the church board in an effort to resolve the matter privately; (3) if the first or second steps do not resolve the matter, then the member or the church board may submit the matter to the membership of the assembly in a special business meeting called for that purpose. Only active voting members of the church shall be permitted to attend such a special business meeting. The decision of a majority of the voting members present at such a meeting shall be final. A member found guilty may be dismissed from membership in the church (Matthew 18:17). However, lesser disciplinary sanctions may be imposed as appropriate, depending on the circumstances of each case.

Members who are under discipline by this assembly forfeit and waive the right to resign from membership in this assembly. Resignations from membership are possible only by those members in good standing who are not under any disciplinary action.

The Nature and Purposes of Discipline
Discipline is an exercise of scriptural authority for which the church is responsible. The aims of discipline are that God may be honored, that the purity and

welfare of the ministry may be maintained, and that those under discipline may be brought to repentance and restoration."

Any church could simply put such a policy in their by-laws, implement it and help awaken the sinning member, protect the church's reputation and honor the Lord.

THE TRAGIC RESULTS OF
A CHURCH'S NEGLECT

Mr. Clinton might well have been delivered from his personal demons and the disgrace on his presidency. But due to his church's total neglect, Clinton continued on until his indulgences became his master and a whole nation suffered for it. While some view the Bible's plan as "harsh" treatment, its purpose is to help the wanderer. We do not consider it harsh when a doctor orders a heart patient off his job until he has received proper treatment and his health is restored. Likewise, it should not be considered harsh when a church orders a man out of its fellowship until he has morally recovered and is able to conduct himself in a way that does not dishonor Jesus Christ.

Immanuel Baptist Church's flagrant refusal to discipline its most famous member makes it responsible for Mr. Clinton continuing to plunge deeper and deeper into a moral abyss. Year after year, women have told of sexual misconduct with Bill Clinton. Yet, the church has ignored the charges. While the congregation sang "Rescue the Perishing," it made no serious effort to "rescue" this man. A church has turned its back, a staff has made it a best-kept secret and a great man has slipped down the slopes of sin, disgraced his family and ruined his reputation.

Chapter Twelve

THE LYNCH MOB
AND WITCH BURNERS

Bishop T. D. Jakes, one of the most prominent pastor's in America, proclaimed "The spirit of the lynch mob" was at large—one that "had led to the burning of witches in Salem, the lynching of black people." *The Dallas Morning News*, quotes Jakes as appealing for forgiveness of President Clinton. Jakes was rather exclusive in his cry for forgiveness. There wasn't a word about forgiving Kenneth Starr, a man he equates with the witch burners and black lynchers. Nor did Jakes mention forgiving those long-departed souls who burned witches, or lynched black people. Nor did Jakes ask us to forgive him for his blatant attack on the government's investigators he assails as being as bad as those who lynched black people.

Dorothy Rabinowitz, writing in *The Wall Street Journal*, warns Jakes and the rest of the Clinton forgivers, "Those counseling forgiveness...might pause to recall the fate of Pope Gregory, the reformer who excommunicated Henry IV, the Holy Roman Emperor, a little less than a millennium ago. Henry seeking absolution, begged and did penance before Gregory, who yielded and reinstated him in the church. An act he would in due course regret as he fled for his life, banished, once Henry had re-established power. There is a moral here somewhere."[140] Yes there is. And that moral is beware of forgiving the unrepentant.

GRAHAM BROADCASTS
COMPLETE FORGIVENESS

Rev. Billy Graham announced forgiveness for President Clinton during an interview on the March 5, 1998, *Today Show*, before the President had even admitted to lying or "having an improper relation" with Monica Lewinsky. When Graham was asked if he would forgive the President for his alleged affair with Lewinsky, the evangelist replied, "I forgive him. I don't know what the average person—but, I mean, certainly I forgive him. Because I know the frailty of human nature and I know how hard it is—especially a strong, vigorous young man like he is. And he has such a tremendous personality that I think the ladies just go wild over him....This is just a hard time to be a moral man. This is just a hard time to be president. This is just a difficult time to resist temptation....of course, what's going on now, there's no proof yet to some of the things that President Clinton is accused of. And then if he is guilty, I would forgive him and love him just the same because he's a remarkable man. and he's had a lot of temptations thrown his way and a lot of pressure on him....the pressure on a president today is unbelievable." Following this interview, Katie Couric said of Billy Graham, "He's really an amazing man and he's so comforting."[141]

Rev. Graham gave six reasons for extending forgiveness to the President: first, because it is "human nature" to commit adultery; second because it is especially hard for a "strong, vigorous" young man to resist adultery; third, because the ladies "go wild over him;" fourth, because this is just "a hard time to be a moral man;" fifth because he's a "remarkable" man; and sixth because "pressure on a president today is unbelievable."

THE WHITE HOUSE IS NOT IN HEAVEN

Graham's declaration of absolution for Clinton touched off a firestorm of indignation from the secular and religious worlds. Cal Thomas, in an editorial titled *Billy Graham Should Remember The White House Is Not in Heaven,* responded, "First, in offering Clinton 'forgiveness,' Graham is suggesting there is something to forgive. Clinton has stated publicly he 'never had a sexual relationship with that woman, Ms. Lewinsky.'....So for what exactly is Graham forgiving the president? Is it lying under oath? Is it blanket forgiveness that also covers illegal campaign contributions, purloined FBI files, suborning of perjury and the orchestrated cover-up of these and other 'sins'? "[142]

Radio talk show host Chuck Baldwin said, "On the statement that Dr. Graham would forgive Bill Clinton, let's remember this: there is no forgiveness without repentance! That is endemic to the central teaching of Christian dogma, and nobody knows it better than Billy Graham. He's preached repentance for over fifty years....Forgiveness does not negate the responsibility of the one that has committed the impropriety to seek forgiveness. That's called repentance....Bill Clinton has not done that in any way, shape, manner or form."[143]

"Rev. Billy Graham has gone so far as to offer Clinton his personal pardon, no matter what occurred, while appearing to lay the blame on flirtatious women," said Julia Malone, in *The Atlanta Constitution.* "In offering comfort to the president, some of the keepers of the nation's moral standards are finding themselves in uncomfortably contradictory positions, however."[144]

ANN LANDERS JOINS THE
FORGIVENESS CHORUS

America's spiritual counselor and pop theologian, Ann Landers, echoed the sentiments of the forgiving ministers, saying, "People are much more willing to forgive now. They are more permissive. They are more realistic. This is the way life is. Not all husbands are faithful.... I've been doing this 43 years. The country has been going in this direction for some time. I don't think it's just the Clintons. We're getting to be more forgiving as a people. It's a good thing." Ann Landers knows. Adultery, lying and permissiveness is "the way life is." Facing this fact is "realistic." Though Landers has not received tablets on Mt. Sinai, she espouses moral authority based on the fact she has written newspaper columns for 43 years. Landers' implication is that the reason more people are forgiving, and should be forgiving these days, is because more of them are guilty. Would Landers agree that if more men start beating up their wives, we will realistically become more forgiving of wife-beating?

AFTER THE CONFESSION THE CRY
FOR FORGIVENESS GREW LOUDER

After seven months of dogmatic denials, the President finally admitted that he had misled the public and had engaged in an "improper" relationship with Monica Lewinsky. This was followed by ministers demanding that this end the matter. Their cry for blanket forgiveness has grown so loud that it is deafening.

Rev. Wogaman, pulled off a sermon that would have made Harry Houdini proud. He declared that "facts" about Clinton's behavior can be used to "obscure" the truth. That is like saying, "knowing the facts of how many points each football team scored can made it more difficult to learn which team won." Rev. Wogaman's statement is as hard to understand as Houdini's escape from a straight jacket. He went on to advise his congregation to heed I Corinthians 13, from which he read: "Love is patient, love is kind. ... Love keeps no score of wrongs, does not gloat over other men's sins, but delights in the truth" (I Corinthians 13:4-6).[145] From this text Wogaman preached about a Christian's obligation to forgive Bill Clinton, without addressing Clinton's obligation.

In a letter to Clinton, Rev. Chandler D. Owens offered "prayerful support during what must be a difficult time." He pointed Clinton to John 8:11, in which Jesus told a woman accused of adultery that he did not condemn her and told her "Go, and sin no more."[146] Rev. Owens did not point out that this was only done after the contrite woman declared Jesus to be her "Lord," the one in total control of her life. Also, it was done by Jesus Christ who knows the heart of all and knew she meant it

"We have an obligation this time to say, 'Hey, enough of this already,'" said the Rev. J. Delano Ellis II, presiding bishop of the United Pentecostal Churches of Christ. Ellis told Clinton in a letter that he is in "the community of the forgiven" because Christianity is "a faith of second chances." Ellis and about 200 members of his Cleveland congregation recently spent a day fasting and praying for Clinton, Vice President Al Gore, and their families, "that God would, in His own mercy, vindicate the man and turn this thing around for the good of the nation," Ellis said.[147] The Rev. Ellis assures us God will "vindicate" Mr. Clinton. This means to "exonerate," or to "absolve of all blame."

THE EFFECTS OF THIS TEACHING
ON BILL CLINTON

On Tuesday, January 27, 1998, the *Associated Press* released an article titled, "Clinton drawing comfort from ministers." It said, "As controversy washes over him, President Clinton is finding comfort in the advice of ministers, through prayer with them and in letters and phone calls from clergy pointing him to Bible verses. Ministers say they seek to uplift not only Clinton, but also a shocked and worried nation that is wrestling with allegations that the president had an affair with a former White House intern and tried to cover it up."

Aides said the President appreciated the ministers' efforts. One official, speaking on condition of anonymity, said Clinton was particularly buoyed by the Scripture referrals. The tragedy of the misleading ministerial cries for forgiveness is they have instructed the President that he has done all that is required. He hasn't. Their statement may have buoyed the President, but it interfered with him performing the necessary true repentance and restitution. Their forgiveness was premature.

First, the President has behaved as if the public should forgive him for an adulterous affair without him having to go through the trauma of confessing it. When DNA evidence threatened to prove he was guilty, he went on television and confessed to an "improper relationship" and then attacked Special Prosecutor Kenneth Starr for uncovering it. When a cry arose over him never using the words "forgive me," he went on television and said those two words. When that did not settle the matter, Mr. Clinton went so far as to speak of "repentance and atonement." He even did a version of King

David's confession. David said he was a man with a "broken and contrite heart." Clinton said he was a man with a "broken, but strong heart."

Columnist George F. Will writes, "Whoever is scripting Clinton's various contrition skits misses this point: Serial contrition, carefully calibrated, is oxymoronic. Clinton's current confessional theme, displayed again in the Rose Garden on Friday (December 11, 1998, at the time of the impeachment vote), is: I am ashamed of what I did to conceal behavior I was ashamed of, so now I have nothing to be ashamed of...Clinton, whose self-absorption is the eighth wonder of the world, thinks the current controversy is about the purity of his repentance."[148]

Following an expanded confession at the Presidential Prayer Breakfast, more than 70 Bible scholars signed a statement protesting the "manipulation of religion and the debasing of moral language." A November 26, 1998 Baptist Press release says their six-point statement complained of those who misused religion to help the president avoid punishment, twisting forgiveness to relieve him of responsibility and minimizing the seriousness of Clinton's transgression.

"We believe that serious misunderstandings of repentance and forgiveness are being exploited for political advantage," the document states. "The resulting moral confusion is a threat to the integrity of American religion and to the foundations of a civil society. We fear the religious community is in danger of being called upon to provide authentication for a politically motivated and incomplete repentance that seeks to avert serious consequences for wrongful acts."

The signers represented a broad-based group of evangelicals from many seminaries and other schools. Nearly all were from the left-leaning liberal institutions. These included Princeton Theological Seminary, Fuller Theological Seminary,

Duke University, Princeton Seminary and Wheaton College.

THE FOUR LEVELS OF FORGIVENESS
THAT MUST BE DISTINGUISHED

Through all of this, Clinton's Clergymen have completely obscured what the Bible says about forgiveness and they have left the country very confused. Dorothy Rabinowitz declares Clinton's moral fall has resulted in the establishment of *The International Forgiveness Institute*, "a center of learning in what is now know as forgiveness studies." So far it is a confusing study. Some indicate an apology is not necessary. Others say a true apology is all that is required. Some say apologies make no difference. Others are confused by the implication that if a minister who speaks for God says, "I forgive him," it means God has forgiven him.

Amidst all this confusion, the Bible provides clear guidelines on forgiveness. It explains there are four levels of forgiveness. First, there is personal forgiveness which should be extended to all who wrong us. The Bible says, "Take heed to yourselves: If thy brother trespass against thee, rebuke him; and if he repent, forgive him. And if he trespass against thee seven times in a day, and seven times in a day turn again to thee, saying, I repent; thou shalt forgive him" (Luke 17:3,4). The number one reason for extending forgiveness is that Christ has forgiven us: "And be ye kind one to another, tenderhearted, forgiving one another, even as God for Christ's sake hath forgiven you" (Ephesians 4:32). Forgiveness provides the benefits of lifting the weight of malice and releasing those who forgive from a life of bitterness.

Second, there is parental forgiveness which must be accompanied by corrective discipline. This teaches the child he must stop his bad behavior.

Third, there is governmental forgiveness which must

be accompanied by justice. The traffic cop should forgive me and not carry a grudge against me, but he should give me a ticket for running the red light.

Fourth, there is divine forgiveness. This is not to be confused with the forgiveness granted by a preacher. When a minister grants personal forgiveness, it does not mean that God is forgiving. God's forgiveness requires these three things the Presidential Prophets have not made clear to Mr. Clinton.

1. DIVINE FORGIVENESS REQUIRES
WE CONFESS SINS SPECIFICALLY

First, the Bible says: "If we confess our sins, he is faithful and just to forgive us our sins, and to cleanse us from all unrighteousness" (I John 1:9). To "confess our sins" means we say with God what God says about our sins. "Confess" is a translation of the Greek word *homologeo* (hom-ol-og-eh'-o); according to *Strong's Lexicon* it comes "from a compound of the base of; to assent, i.e. covenant, acknowledge: In the King James Bible it is used to mean...we declare our sin is wrong, it is a horrible evil, it is something we should never have done, nor ever should do again."

Mr. Clinton could render a great service to the nation by naming his sins specifically, condemning the conduct, apologizing for it and vowing he will not do it again.

"Highly public sins by a highly placed official triggers a demoralizing fight between allies who deny or minimize the sin and enemies who call attention to it for the wrong motives," says J. Budziszewski in *World* magazine. "Nothing could be better calculated to spread cynicism throughout the body politic—to convince the citizens that all statesmen lie and all virtue is just a fraud....If the wrongdoer admits to both his enemies and his allies that he has committed a terrible wrong, they can no longer bicker about what he did or whether it matters."[149]

2. DIVINE FORGIVENESS
REQUIRES REPENTANCE

God's forgiveness demands people repent, or turn from their sin: "Repent ye therefore... that your sins may be blotted out, when the times of refreshing shall come from the presence of the Lord" (Acts 3:19).

George Stroup, Professor of Theology at Columbia Theological Seminary in Decatur, Georgia, says, "I guess for many of us the very deep dilemma is in not wanting to be legalistic and judgmental, to argue that God's grace is about forgiveness. On the other hand, how do you keep it from becoming cheap grace where anything goes?"[150] The answer to Stroup's dilemma is you keep God's grace from being cheap by saying there is no forgiveness apart from repentance. God does not forgive until people are willing to turn from their sins.

3. DIVINE FORGIVENESS
REQUIRES THAT WE FORGIVE

Nothing is more emphatically taught about forgiveness than the fact that no one receives forgiveness until he or she is willing to forgive. Christ said: "For if ye forgive men their trespasses, your heavenly Father will also forgive you: But if ye forgive not men their trespasses, neither will your Father forgive your trespasses" (Matthew 6:14,15).

Bill Clinton made an appeal for forgiveness from Jews, whose religion requires much more than asking for forgiveness. Clinton told the Jewish clergy assembled at the White House for a Yom Kippur breakfast that he was admitting sins and saying he needed to turn from them. In his beautifully worded statement, Clinton said, "For leaves, birds and animals, turning comes instinctively. But for us, turning does not come so easily. It takes an act of will for us to make a turn. It means breaking old habits. It means admitting that we have been wrong, and this is never easy. It means losing face. It means starting all over again. And this is always painful. It means saying I am sorry. It means recognizing that we have the ability to change. These things are terribly hard to do. But unless we turn, we will be trapped forever in yesterday's ways."[151]

Rabbi Steven Lebow, Reform Rabbi of Cobb County Atlanta's Temple Kol Emeth, in response to Clinton's beautifully worded message, said: "What Jewish philosophy says is that God can only forgive you for what you've done in relation to God. In order to achieve atonement with fellow human beings, you have to go to them and say what you've done wrong and ask them to forgive you."[152] In Clinton's Christian faith you have to go much farther. You must forgive those who have wronged you.

Jesus Christ taught us to pray: "Forgive us our debts, as we forgive our debtors" (Matthew 6:12). He ordered that when we pray we must forgive: "And when ye stand praying, forgive, if ye have ought against any: that your Father also which is in heaven may forgive you your trespasses" (Mark 11:25).

Jesus illustrated the necessity of forgiving in this poignant story: "Then came Peter to him, and said, Lord, how oft shall my brother sin against me, and I forgive him? till seven times? Jesus saith unto him, I say not unto thee, Until seven times: but, Until seventy times seven. Therefore is the kingdom of heaven likened unto a certain king, which would take account of his servants. And when he had begun to reckon, one was brought unto him, which owed him ten thousand talents. But forasmuch as he had not to pay, his lord commanded him to be sold, and his wife, and children, and all that he had, and payment to be made. The servant therefore fell down, and worshipped him, saying, Lord, have patience with me, and I will pay thee all. Then the lord of that servant was moved with compassion, and loosed him, and forgave him the debt.

"But the same servant went out, and found one of his fellowservants, which owed him an hundred pence: and he laid hands on him, and took him by the throat, saying, Pay me that thou owest. And his fellowservant fell down at his feet, and besought him, saying, Have patience with me, and I will pay thee all. And he would not: but went and cast him into prison, till he should pay the debt.

"So when his fellow servants saw what was done, they were very sorry, and came and told unto their lord all that was done. Then his lord, after that he had called him, said unto him, O thou wicked servant, I forgave thee all that debt, because thou desiredst me: Shouldest not thou also have had compassion on thy fellowservant, even as I had pity on thee? And his lord was wroth, and delivered him to the tormentors, till he should pay all that was due unto him. So likewise shall my heavenly Father do also unto you, if ye from your hearts forgive not every one his brother their trespasses" (Matthew 18:21-35). This is emphatic. God does not forgive those who do not forgive others.

With all the vicious enemies Clinton has, there is a bountiful field for him to practice forgiveness. Newt Gingrich, R-Georgia, called Clinton "a criminal;" Majority Leader Dick Armey, R-Texas, called his actions "treasonous;" Representative Dan Burton, R-Indiana, called him "a scumbag;" and Sen. Jesse Helms, R-North Carolina, warned Clinton that if he came to his state it would be at his own risk![153]

St. Augustine, the 5th-century bishop, wrote in his "Confessions" that people such as Mr. Clinton would be well-advised to practice the Bible command to forgive, not only to be forgiven, but also to escape a load of hatred: "As if any enemy could be more hurtful than the hatred with which he is incensed against him; or could wound more deeply him whom he persecutes, than he wounds his own soul by his enmity."

The Presidential Prophets have absolutely buried the need for Clinton to grant forgiveness. They cry that Clinton has done all that is required because he has confessed his sins and said he has repented. No! He must also forgive his enemies and call off his attack dogs.

FORGIVENESS DOESN'T EXEMPT US
FROM SIN'S CONSEQUENCES

Rev. Jesse Jackson attacked Rev. Jerry Falwell on the August 22, CNN show. Jackson quoted Scripture on forgiveness and asked Falwell why he would not forgive President Clinton. Falwell contended that forgiveness was one thing, but removing him from office was something else—that was about consequences.[154]

The big cry for the forgiveness of the President has mostly been about letting him continue in office; or exempting him from consequences. The Clinton Clergymen need to remember that Jesus Christ forgave a thief on the cross, but He did not voice a word about freeing the thief from his death penalty. Forgiveness doesn't remove consequences.

Some ministers and some members of the media have tried to label anyone who wants the President to pay a price for his sins as "unforgiving." *The Atlanta Journal-Constitution* did a feature article entitled, "Searching for Forgiveness." Some religious leaders call for judgment on Clinton while others express willingness to put scandal behind them."[155] The article divided ministers into two groups: those who want punishment and those who want to forgive. By exclusion, the implication was if you want the President to pay for his wrongs, you have not forgiven him. The article did not allow a possibility of wanting both. The article pits a Jewish judge against a Christian forgiver. Rabbi Steven Lebow said his faith requires "confessing, apologizing to those who have been wronged and attempting to make restitution." On the other side of the fence, the *Atlanta Journal-Constitution* article quotes Max Lucado, a San Antonio minister and author, as saying, "what makes Christianity different in my perspective is Jesus gives us a way to have our sins taken away. First of all that gives us assurance—you, me and President Clinton—that I confess my sins to Christ and they're taken away. My recourse is to never deny sin, but to always confess sin."[156]

While God ordained that Christians minister forgiveness, He also ordained that governments minister justice: "For rulers are not a terror to good works, but to the evil....For he is the minister of God to thee for good. But if thou do that which is evil, be afraid; for he beareth not the sword in vain: for he is the minister of God, a revenger to execute wrath upon him that doeth evil" (Romans 13:3,4). God holds people responsible for forgiving. He holds governments responsible for justly punishing.

The real error in publicly extending forgiveness is the implication that forgiveness means absolving the erring party of all consequences for his wrong. The logic of this choir of ministers offering forgiveness to Mr. Clinton is: (1) The Bible says we should forgive sinners. (2) Forgiveness means we do not want to see the sinner suffer for his wrong. (3) Therefore the Bible says we should treat Mr. Clinton as if he had never committed adultery and let him stay in office.

The error in this reasoning lies in the second point, that forgiveness means we do not want the sinner to suffer. My daddy always forgave me when I was bad, but he never failed to use his heavy leather belt on my posterior. Rev. Lester Buice, a friend of mine went to a jail in Atlanta and forgave the man who raped his daughter-in-law and stomped her to death. Then he asked the judge to give the man the death penalty. Forgiving a person means we will not carry bitterness against them. It does not mean that we do not approve of justice. Forgiveness and justice are perfectly compatible.

While Dr. Billy Graham was offering forgiveness, his son, Franklin, demanded Clinton's removal from office: "For the sake of the country, the best thing he can do is quietly resign...Let (Vice President) Al Gore pardon him and get it off the front pages and into history."[157]

Charles W. Colson, who served under President Nixon, says, "As many people may remember, I've had some personal experience with this. twenty-five years ago, I became a Christian in the midst of Watergate. I asked forgiveness for my sins, and I knew God forgave me. But I also knew I had to pay the consequences for breaking the law. I pleaded guilty—and went to prison."[158]

Chapter Thirteen

WHY BILL CLINTON'S FAITH DIDN'T WORK

At the root of Clinton's moral failure lies conflicting, confusing teachings about religious faith that would be enough to bewilder even a president. The Clinton Clergymen have said you can believe in Jesus and ignore the rest of the Bible. Then they have said you do not even have to believe everything about Jesus, just pick out what is reasonable and forget the rest. If this is not confusing enough, they have also said you can just believe in the god of your choice and it doesn't matter if you have ever heard of Jesus Christ.

It is amazing that these ministers can stand in a pulpit with a Bible in their hands and hold a straight face while they deny its truths. What the Clinton Clergymen have done to the Bible's teaching about faith would be hilarious if it were not destroying the souls of people. Those who listen to them will, like President Clinton, end up with a faith that does not work.

BELIEVE WHAT THE BIBLE SAYS ABOUT JESUS AND IGNORE THE REST

Clinton's longtime Arkansas pastor, Rev. W. O. Vaught, taught you can believe what the Bible said about Jesus and you don't need to worry about anything else the Bible teaches regarding salvation. He declared,

> "The clearest statement in all the Word of God of the plan of salvation is found in Acts 16:31 when Paul and Silas said to the Philippian jailer, 'Believe on the Lord Jesus Christ and thou shalt be saved.' This is precisely what every man must do to be saved and no matter how many other things we attempt to attach to salvation, faith in Jesus Christ is the only thing necessary. This very same emphasis is given in Genesis 15:6 where the conversion of Abraham is recorded. This verse says, 'And he believed in the Lord: and he counted it to him for righteousness.' A little more accurate reading of the Hebrew says, 'And he had believed [possibly as much as 40 or 50 years earlier] in the Lord: and he [God the Father] counted it to him for righteousness.' Here is belief plus nothing. However, man is of such nature that he makes himself believe he has to do something, he has to make changes in his life, he has to feel sorry for his sins, he has to change the direction of his life, and only if he will do all these things can he turn to Christ and be saved."[159]

Vaught proposes a real deal. You can believe in Jesus and you do not abandon your sins, admit your sins are wrong, or even feel sorry for yours sins. Just believe and you have it made. Rev. Vaught's passage says a jailer asked Paul and

Silas, "Sirs, what must I do to be saved?" They replied, "Believe on the Lord Jesus Christ and thou shalt be saved." This is the only recorded instance of anyone asking New Testament Christians what to do in order to be saved. The answer was very clear. "Believe on the Lord Jesus Christ." Furthermore, it is promised with assurance, "Thou shalt be saved." Vaught is absolutely right when he says faith is enough, if faith believes the right things. When the Auca Indians believed sacrificing a young virgin would bring them the blessings of their God, they believed. But, they did not believe the right thing.

The passage in Acts explains you must believe three things regarding the Son of God.

First, you must believe on Him as your "Lord," or Master. It requires that you trust Him to control your life—to rule over you. A person must be willing to be the servant of Christ. When he is willing, Christ comes into his heart, gives him His power, and makes him able. True saving faith brings us to the point at which we are willing. Jesus called on the wealthy tax collector to believe in Him by simply saying to Matthew: "Follow me." Following Christ meant leaving his business. It was hard, but Christ demanded that Matthew believed He was "the Lord" whom he must obey and follow. Matthew demonstrated his faith when he left all and followed Him, passing the test of genuine faith. Believing in Christ as Lord is another way of stating repentance of sin.

An extremely liberal critic of the Bible has now turned his guns on himself and other skeptics like those who have coached Bill Clinton. With an honesty that is startling, Gerd Ludemann, Professor of New Testament and Director of the Institute of Early Christian Studies at Gottingen University in Germany, declared he is an atheist and that liberal Protestant preachers are actually closet atheists. Mr. Ludemann offered this startling observation: "I don't think Christians know what they mean when they proclaim Jesus as Lord of the World. That is a massive claim. If you took that seriously, you would probably have to be a fundamentalist. If you can't be a fundamentalist, then you should give up Christianity for the sake of honesty." Dr. R. Albert Mohler says, "Professor Ludemann is now a formidable foe of liberal theology, but he is also one of its victims."[160] Professor Ludemann is telling the truth. The Bible demands we either recognize Christ as Lord, or give up the Christian faith.

Second, we must believe in Him as "Jesus" our "Saviour"—the one who died and rose again to save us from our sins. Matthew 1:21 says, "Thou shalt call His name JESUS: for He shall save His people from their sins." Christ paid the wages of death required for our sins so we would not have to pay for them. To believe, the Bible requires that we depend on Jesus for our salvation. This disallows believing in our own good works, other gods, or our own faith to atone for our sins. When President Clinton spoke at his 1998 prayer breakfast about making "atonement" for his sins, it raised a question. Have his ministers explained to him that Jesus Christ made the only atonement for sin that can ever be accepted by God?

Third, we must believe in "Christ," as the "anointed" one. Christ was anointed to be Priest and King. This was the name the prophets used when referring to the promised Messiah. He is the Priest, the one who made intercession between man and God. He is the King who rules over God's eternal Kingdom. Saving faith trusts Christ as the true Messiah, the one God has anointed as Priest and King of God's Kingdom.

In 1996, I was in London's Hyde Park, the Super Bowl of debate, with about 30,000 who assembled on a sunny Sunday afternoon. One man carried a double 6-foot sign saying "Christian Atheist." When I challenged him, he said he believes in Jesus as an ethical example. But, he does not believe in His divinity. This man has faith in Jesus Christ, but it will not save him. I pointed out to the gentleman that he was in a rather strange position. Either Jesus Christ was the Son of God He claimed to be or he was a lying impostor. If He is not God's Son, he is certainly no ethical example.

Saving faith requires as its object the belief that Jesus is the Lord, the Saviour, and the King. When people sincerely believe these three things, they are saved.

BELIEVE WHATEVER YOU WANT ABOUT JESUS AND IGNORE THE BIBLE

Rev. Wogaman cuts Clinton a better deal than Vaught. He preaches that you don't have to believe all the stuff in the Bible about Jesus. Just pick the things that seem reasonable to you. Wogaman chooses to throw away the part about Jesus being born of a virgin. He says it is expecting too much to ask anyone to believe all the Bible because it contains, "contradictions...[and] even questionable moral teaching?"[161]

BELIEVE IN WHATEVER GOD YOU CHOOSE AND IGNORE JESUS

If Clinton is not confused enough by this, Dr. Billy Graham has an even better deal. Clinton does not have to believe anything in the Bible, or anything about Jesus. It is not essential to ever see a Bible, or hear the name of Jesus Christ. The most popular preacher in America, the man who led Bill Clinton to his profession of faith in Christ and the man who has had the longest spiritual influence on Clinton, says you do not even have to believe in Christ. Just believe in some god. Any god will do: Jesus, Mohammed, or Buddha. Here is what Clinton's father in the faith, Dr. Billy Graham, told Dr. Robert

Schuller's national TV audience on May 31 and June 8, 1997:

Dr. Graham: "I think everybody that loves Christ, or knows Christ, whether they're conscious of it or not, they're members of the Body of Christ...And that's what God is doing today, He's calling people out of the world for His name, whether they come from the Muslim world, or the Buddhist world, or the Christian world or the non-believing world, they are members of the Body of Christ because they've been called by God.

"They may not even know the name of Jesus but they know in their hearts that they need something that they don't have, and they turn to the only light that they have, and I think that they are saved, and that they're going to be with us in Heaven."

Dr. Schuller: "I hear you saying that it's possible for Jesus Christ to come into human hearts and soul and life, even if they've been born in darkness and have never had exposure to the Bible. Is that a correct interpretation of what you're saying?"

Dr. Graham: "Yes, it is, because I believe that. I've met people in various parts of the world in tribal situations, that they have never seen a Bible or heard about a Bible, and never heard of Jesus, but they've believed in their hearts that there was a God, and they've tried to live a life that was quite apart from the surrounding community in which they lived."

Dr. Schuller: "I'm so thrilled to hear you say this. There's a wideness in God's mercy."

Dr. Graham: "There is. There definitely is."[162]

This is very confusing. Here Rev. Billy Graham contradicted the basic truths that he has spent his life preaching—the truths he built his ministry upon. Dr. Billy Graham told his audience during his great New York City crusade in the 60s:

> "Jesus said, 'The road is narrow; the gate is narrow.' And He said, 'If you're going to go the narrow road that leads to eternal life, you'll have to go through the narrow gate.' Now, what is that gate? Jesus said, 'I am the way. I am the door. By me if any man enter in he shall be saved." Jesus said, "Don't try to come some other way. That's like a robber." He said, 'There is only one door. There is one gate. I am the way. I am the truth. I am the light.' I am the way to Heaven. You have to come by me.'
> "Now you say, 'Billy, I can't accept that. I want to go to Heaven...but I just don't want to come by the way of Jesus.' Well, I am sorry, but I cannot compromise at that point. I have to go by the rule book. I cannot bargain. I have no authority from the Bible to bargain with your soul. I have no authority to lower the standards. Jesus said, 'I am the door. By me if any man enter in he shall be saved.'"[163]

Morning anchor Katie Couric talked with Dr. Graham on the March 5, 1998 *Today Show* about his memory. She asked Dr. Graham if "Parkinson's affects your short-term memory just a bit." He replied, "Well, yes. Some people say it does, and some say it doesn't. I've talked to people who have it, who tell me it does. And it affects mine.

Something does. I don't know...it may be old age."[164] In all fairness to Dr. Graham, it may be that he has forgotten what the Bible says and what he has preached for so many years that has transformed so many thousands of people.

TRUE FAITH MUST COME
FROM THE HEART-NOT THE HEAD

Dr. W. O. Vaught ignored the fact that genuine faith comes from the heart and endures. He said, "Let us take Mr. X as an illustration. Mr. X believed in Christ, joined the church and was baptized. For quite some time he lived what appeared to be a very consecrated and happy Christian life. Later Mr. X began to give up his church loyalty, was less and less regular in church attendance, and finally dropped out completely, saying he never planned to go back again. Quite often the superficial observer will say, 'See, Mr. X really wasn't genuinely saved in the first place. But if he was, then he has lost his salvation.' What does the Scripture say to erroneous thinking of this kind?"[165] Well, if by abandoning church attendance Vaught implies abandoning Jesus, it is by no means "erroneous" thinking. It is exactly what Jesus taught.

Jesus Christ presented a parable about a sower to show that true faith endures because it come from deep within the heart. In the parable, a sower throws some seed among rocks. Christ explained, "They on the rock are they, which, ...receive the word with joy; and these have no root, which for a while believe, and in time of temptation fall away" (Luke 8:13). They "believed" for a while, but fell away when temptation arose. Their faith was faulty. Christ contrasted this with the seed which fell on proper soil: "But that on the good ground are they, which in an honest and good heart, having heard the word, keep it, and bring forth fruit with patience" (Luke 8:15). Their faith is genuine. It is embedded in an "honest and good heart." Its distinguishing mark is it endures.

The Bible tells of a man named Simon who heard the gospel and "believed." Still he was going to "perish" because his heart was "not right" with God: "But when they believed Philip preaching the things concerning the kingdom of God, and the name of Jesus Christ, they were baptized, both men and women. Then Simon himself believed also: and when he was baptized, he continued with Philip, and wondered, beholding the miracles and signs which were done...And when Simon saw that through laying on of the apostles' hands the Holy Ghost was given, he offered them money, Saying, Give me also this power, that on whomsoever I lay hands, he may receive the Holy Ghost. But Peter said unto him, Thy money perish with thee, because thou hast thought that the gift of God may be purchased with money. Thou hast neither part nor lot in this matter: for thy heart is not right in the sight of God. Repent therefore of this thy wickedness, and pray God, if perhaps the thought of thine heart may be forgiven thee" (Acts 8:12, 13, 18-22). He "believed," yet he was going to "perish." The reason was his "heart was not right." The man's faith came from his head, not his heart.

The Clinton Clergy have evidently failed to explain to the President the vast difference between a simple mental assent and a genuine heart trust. Mental assent says "I believe that a hot air balloon can go around the world." A deep heart trust says, "I will get in it."

The Presidential Prophets would have served the President well if they had taught him what wonderful, victorious things can come to those who properly believe. The

Bible promises, "But as many as received him, to them gave he power to become the sons of God, even to them that believe on his name" (John 1:12). This is the power of true faith that frees true believers from the shackles of lusts. This is the power of a faith that has not been required by the Clinton Clergy. This is the power that could have delivered Bill Clinton and prevented the scandal.

Chapter Fourteen

JAMES CARVILLE
BECOMES A PREACHER

James Carville, a Clinton campaign strategist, has turned preacher and theologian. His new book, *The Horse He Rode in On*, deals with some interesting concepts of judgment and hell. Carville confesses it is a subject he prefers to stay away from: "The way I figure it, why do I want to read about hell in this life when I'll be getting so much of it in the next?"[166] Carville says, "I've read a quote by Dante that puts this whole sex investigation in perspective. In the *Inferno*, the Italian poet wrote, 'Eternal Justice weighs the sins of the hot blooded and the cold hearted on different scales.'" Carville now begins to preach like a man with a clear revelation: "In my mind, an indiscretion here and an indiscretion there will never amount to a tenth of cruelty. A passionate indiscretion will never be judged in the same light as the sins of the cold-hearted."[167]

Based on the supreme authority of "my mind," Carville portrays the warm-hearted sins of Bill Clinton as not "a tenth" as bad as the "cold-hearted cruelty" of Kenneth Starr.[168] So if Clinton has to suffer in hell for his warm-hearted sex sins, Kenneth Starr is going to have to suffer ten times as much for investigating Clinton. When Carville spoke about hell it brought to mind Cal Thomas' comment, "When lawyers talk sin and preachers talk politics, surely the demons in hell rejoice."

The week after I read this book by Carville, I spoke with him on an airplane going from Atlanta into Baton Rouge. Among other things, I told him, "At least you had the guts to use the word none of the Presidential Prophets dare to utter— *hell*." Carville froze. He showed no interest in pursuing the subject.

I had trouble understanding this prolific talker being stone silent about hell until I read *a USA Today* editorial on hell the following week. In it William R. Mattox, Jr. said, "Try to engage people...in a serious conversation about hell, and they'll give you a snooty, raised-eyebrow sort of look that says, 'Excuse me, but don't you know it is uncouth to talk about hell in polite conversation?'"[169]

Carville isn't the only one who freezes at the subject of hell. We haven't heard any of the Presidential Prophets preaching on the subject. Hell is a subject Jesus Christ used over and over to persuade sinners to straighten up, but not the Clinton Clergy. "Why is our society so schizophrenic about hell?" asks Mattox. "For example, how is it that 'hell' is one of the most commonly used words in the English language, yet one of the least-talked-about? I mean, go into any sports locker room or military training facility or college night club and you'll hear people use the word 'hell' in all sorts of ways—as an interjection, an adjective, a noun."[170] But no one wants to discuss it, particularly the liberal clergymen.

Jesus Christ said if some part of your body causes you to sin—cut it off!: "Ye have heard that it was said by them of old time, Thou shalt not commit adultery: But I say unto you, That whosoever looketh on a woman to lust after her hath committed adultery with her already in his heart. And if thy right eye offend thee, pluck it out, and cast it from thee: for it is profitable for thee that one of thy members should perish, and not that thy whole body should be cast into hell. And if thy right hand offend thee, cut it off, and cast it from thee: for it is profitable for thee that one of thy members should perish, and not that thy whole body should be cast into hell" (Matthew 5:27-30).

Cal Thomas, writing on September 15, 1998 about the lack of "hellfire and brimstone" preachers in Washington, said, "Watching President Clinton being 'baptized' with forgiveness by a carefully chosen group of theologically and politically liberal clergy Friday recalled a similar event 25 years ago. Richard Nixon held Sunday 'morning-worship' services in the White House....As a young reporter, I covered these strangely sterile events, which were devoid of hellfire and brimstone and any criticism of Nixon's Vietnam or domestic policies. That's because, like Friday's (Clinton prayer breakfast) liberal conclave, the guests were carefully screened. All presidents, regardless of party, love to wrap themselves in men (and women) of the cloth, especially when their presidencies are unraveling."[171]

Sir Winston Churchill provided a prophetic insight into the cause of President Clinton's moral fall when he said if there was more hell in the pulpit, there would be less hell in the pew. If there had been more hell in the pulpits of the President's Prophets, Mr. Clinton's conduct might have been radically changed.

HELL IS A STRONG MOTIVATION
THAT COULD HAVE SAVED CLINTON

Clinton has been denied a powerful motivation to repentance by a group of preachers who refuse to mention hell. Fear is a legitimate restraint used by society to combat drunk driving, unprotected sex, and drugs. Posters and TV public service spots show us pictures of bloody wrecks that killed drunk drivers. We hear tragic horror stories of unprotected sex resulting in the agony of AIDS. "Know before you go" ads tell frightening stories of foreign arrests for drug possession. People who care about the welfare of others use the proven motivation of fear. But compromising preachers are real proud of the fact that they do not use fear to "scare people" into repenting of their sins. These "no-hellers," as Rev. Williard Tallman used to call them, do not care enough about the souls of people like Bill Clinton to stand up and tell them the truth.

The Clinton's Clergymen run for the Bible when they want to preach that we should forgive the President, but they run from the Bible when it mentions hell. Yet the Scriptures the President's Prophets preach from plainly say, "And of some have compassion, making a difference: And others save with fear, pulling them out of the fire" (Jude 1:22,23). The Clinton Clergymen are disobeying this command and depriving the President of a powerful motivation to abandon his sins. Their preaching is exactly what Cal Thomas says: "sterile" and "devoid of hellfire and brimstone."

Author Jerry Walls, in his book, *Hell: The Logic of Damnation,* declares that a person cannot believe in God without also believing in a hell for those who do not want God. Walls says, "If there is no God, no Heaven, no Hell, there simply is no persuasive reason to be moral."[172]

"Several years ago, Great Britain's secretary of State for education and science, John Patten, argued that crime in the United Kingdom was rising because the fear of hell was declining. Patten's argument wasn't exactly well received in jolly ol' England," writes Mattox.[173] Neither is it well received by the Presidential Prophets.

WHAT CLINTON'S CLERGYMEN
FAILED TO TELL HIM ABOUT HELL

Clinton's Clergymen are refusing to follow Jesus Christ's example of using hell as a regular part of His preaching. Jesus told of unrepentant sinners burning in the flames of hell in every major discourse. If a preacher is going to follow Christ, he has no choice but to preach on hell and to preach on it just the way Jesus did. Ministers who try to take the fire out of hell and explain it away have departed from the example of Jesus.

There is reason to believe that the President might have responded to a sermon on hell. He believes in life beyond the grave, and that we receive the rewards there for what we have done on earth. In his high school graduation benediction, Clinton prayed that the class would, "know and care what is right and wrong, so that we can be victorious in this life and rewarded in the next."[174] He just has not heard the truth about what the rewards for sin will be in the next life.

David Maraniss recalls a flight with President Clinton in 1992. After asking him what his deepest moral challenge was, Clinton responded, "the failures of daily life that often grind people down and leave them so disappointed with themselves." Later, the President added that he and Hillary had been talking more about what it meant to live a good life and what life after death was like. Maraniss asked whether

Clinton believes in life after death and Clinton replied, "Yeah, I have to. I need a second chance."[175] Again, in all the years of listening to preachers, the President does not understand there is no second chance after death. Jesus called hell "everlasting fire" (Matthew 25:41) and "everlasting punishment" (Matthew 25:46).

Clinton's Clergymen should have told the President that God has created a special place of fire and brimstone for sinful rulers. He even lit it with the breath of his fury: "For Tophet is ordained of old; yea, for the king it is prepared; he hath made it deep and large: the pile thereof is fire and much wood; the breath of the LORD, like a stream of brimstone, doth kindle it" (Isaiah 30:33).

These political prophets should make their audiences aware that the fire in hell will never go out: "Whose fan is in his hand, and he will throughly purge his floor, and gather his wheat into the garner; but he will burn up the chaff with unquenchable fire" (Matthew 3:12).

Why don't we hear the Washington clergymen describing how men weep and gnash their teeth in pain? Jesus said, "And I say unto you, That many shall come from the east and west, and shall sit down with Abraham, and Isaac, and Jacob, in the kingdom of heaven. But the children of the kingdom shall be cast out into outer darkness: there shall be weeping and gnashing of teeth" (Matthew 8:11,12). "Cast him into outer darkness; there shall be weeping and gnashing of teeth" (Matthew 22:13).

The preachers should be warning Clinton not to be afraid of losing the presidency, his power or even his life, but to fear losing his soul in hell. Jesus said: "And fear not them which kill the body, but are not able to kill the soul: but rather fear him which is able to destroy both soul and body in hell" (Matthew 10:28).

The President should be made aware that hell is a furnace of fire: "The Son of man shall send forth his angels, and they shall gather out of his kingdom all things that offend, and them which do iniquity; And shall cast them into a furnace of fire: there shall be wailing and gnashing of teeth...So shall it be at the end of the world: the angels shall come forth, and sever the wicked from among the just, And shall cast them into the furnace of fire: there shall be wailing and gnashing of teeth" (Matthew 13:41,42,49,50).

Hell is intended for the Devil and his fallen angels: "Then shall he say also unto them on the left hand, Depart from me, ye cursed, into everlasting fire, prepared for the devil and his angels" (Matthew 25:41). God does not want to take away our right to choose and turn us into robots. If we are determined to go to hell, He will allow us the choice to do so.

Jesus Christ is the only real authority on the subject of hell. He is the only one to die and rise again to die no more. Christ gave this story of eternity, using proper names to indicate it is no mere parable: "And in hell he lift up his eyes, being in torments, and seeth Abraham afar off, and Lazarus in his bosom. And he cried and said, Father Abraham, have mercy on me, and send Lazarus, that he may dip the tip of his finger in water, and cool my tongue; for I am tormented in this flame. But Abraham said, Son, remember that thou in thy lifetime receivedst thy good things, and likewise Lazarus evil things: but now he is comforted, and thou art tormented. And beside all this, between us and you there is a great gulf fixed: so that they which would pass from hence to you cannot; neither can they pass to us, that would come from thence. Then he said, I pray thee therefore, father, that thou wouldest send him to my father's house: For I have five brethren; that he may testify unto them, lest they also come into this place of torment. Abraham saith unto him, They have Moses and the prophets; let them hear them" (Luke 16:23-29).

Many modern clergymen are working frantically to improve on Jesus' words by taking the fire out of hell. The Church of England has rejected the idea of hell as a place of fire and screams of unending agony. Instead, it now declares hell is the annihilation of all who reject the love of God. "Whether there be any who do so choose, only God knows," said a report by the church's Doctrinal Commission. The Commission rejects what it calls "the medieval vision of the underworld" as a harmful teaching: "Christians have professed appalling theologies which made God into a sadistic monster and left searing psychological scars on many." The report said, "Hell is not eternal torment, but it is the final and irrevocable, choosing of that which is opposed to God so completely and so absolutely that the only end is total non-being."[176]

Rev. Billy Graham, the President's trusted friend, presents hell in a very inoffensive way. He says the fire, the darkness and the thirst are figurative words, which really mean separation from God: "Whatever Hell may mean, it is separation from God. Now there are *three words* that Jesus used constantly to describe it. One is called *Fire*....Could it be that the fire Jesus talked about is an eternal search for God that is never quenched?[177]

"He used the word darkness...There again, the darkness is separation from God. God is light...The third word that Jesus used is death—the second death to the soul, separation from God."[178]

A fireless hell where the punishment is merely separation from God holds no terror for those with no desire to know God, or be united with Him. They prefer to live without God here. There is no reason to think they would want to live with Him in eternity.

James A. Stewart, the powerful author and mission-ary, cried, "Oh, that God would give us weeping prophets once again! Oh, that He would give us a new generation of young men and young women who have this agony and this burden for lost souls! I think of Paul who, in saying farewell to the elders of Ephesus, could remind his hearers that day and night, for many a long month, he had been weeping in their midst. As Mr. Whitefield used to say to his great congrega-tions, 'If you won't weep for yourselves, dear sinners on the way to hell, then I'll have to weep for you' Then he would break out into uncontrollable weeping."[179]

The political prophets that crowd around the President have no such concern for the welfare of Clinton's soul. Stewart points out how modern preachers have changed: "The prophets of old called their messages burdens. In the old-fashioned evangelism, God's people had an agony over lost souls...Before I can begin preaching, I myself am weeping. Oh yes, that is the true way of revival. Jeremiah was the weeping prophet. 'Oh, that my head were waters,' he cried, 'and my eyes a fountain of tears, that I might weep, day and night for the slain of the daughter of my people.' David the Psalmist says, in the 119th Psalm, 'Rivers of water run down my eyes because they keep not Thy Word.'"[180]

MONICA LEWINSKY'S SECRET

Bill Clinton may have an intimate knowledge of Mon-ica Lewinsky and other promiscuous women. But there re-mains a deep secret about them very few understand. Wise Solomon wrote, "A foolish woman is clamorous: she is simple, and knoweth nothing." She goes about calling, "passengers who go right on their ways: Whoso is simple, let him turn in hither: and as for him that wanteth understanding, she saith to him, Stolen waters are sweet, and bread eaten in secret is pleasant. But he knoweth not that the dead are there; and that her guests are in the depths of hell" (Proverbs 9:13-18). This is Monica's secret.

The Clinton Clergy have addressed the question, "Who should be impeached." But they have ignored the far more important question asked in Isaiah 33:14: "Who among us shall dwell with the devouring fire? Who among us shall dwell with everlasting burnings?"

WHY FUNERAL SERMONS AVOID HELL

For a small fee, a funeral director can always obtain a hireling minister who will be delighted to preach a funeral sermon that puts an adulterer inside the pearly gates. This may give assurance to the family, but it is a cruel, false assurance. It is as vicious as telling parents their child is just fine after he has been killed in an automobile wreck. Time will strip away the fantasy and make the tragedy of reality all the more horrid for the loved ones of adulterers.

Ministers neglect the responsibility to make it clear that the majority of people are going to hell. Only a "few" (less than half) people will travel the narrow way to heaven: "Enter ye in at the strait gate: for wide is the gate, and broad is the way, that leadeth to destruction, and many there be which go in thereat: Because strait is the gate, and narrow is the way, which leadeth unto life, and few there be that find it" (Matthew 7:13,14). Stop and ask yourself if you have ever heard one of the Clinton Clergymen conduct a funeral in which there was the slightest hint that the deceased might be in hell. Aren't the deceased always portrayed as being in heaven?

Many modern minds reject the idea of the punishment of hell because they feel it does not fit the crime of adultery. Yet, the Bible declares in Jude 1:7 that this is exactly what the punishment is: "Even as Sodom and Gomorrha, and the cities about them in like manner, giving themselves over to fornication, and going after strange flesh, are set forth for an example, suffering the vengeance of eternal fire." And Revelation's list of the damned includes the sexually immoral: "But the fearful, and unbelieving, and the abominable, and murderers, and whoremongers, and sorcerers, and idolaters, and all liars, shall have their part in the lake which burneth with fire and brimstone: which is the second death" (Revelation 21:8).

The American public runs from the idea of seeing a president put in jail. The thought of someone in such a high position going to hell is absolutely unthinkable. Yet the Bible says that even the high and mighty angels who sinned will go to hell: "God spared not the angels that sinned, but cast them down to hell, and delivered them into chains of darkness, to be reserved unto judgment" (II Peter 2:4).

The Bible vividly portrays what happens to poor deceived souls, "The same shall drink of the wine of the wrath of God, which is poured out without mixture into the cup of his indignation; and he shall be tormented with fire and brimstone in the presence of the holy angels, and in the presence of the Lamb: And the smoke of their torment ascendeth up for ever and ever: and they have no rest day nor night" (Revelation 14:10,11).

And what about the man who stood up and misled the people—the false prophet?"And the beast was taken, and with him the false prophet...These both were cast alive into a lake of fire burning with brimstone" (Revelation 19:20).

Oxford author C.S. Lewis declared that no one ever goes to heaven deservingly—and no one ever goes to hell unwillingly. Jerry Wall makes it simple, saying heaven is for sinners who want to spend eternity with God. Hell is for sinners who want to spend eternity apart from God.

William Mattox closed his *USA Today* editorial on hell

by relating a conversation "with a sometimes-snooty (and always hip) friend of mine. When he sensed that our conversation was headed straight to hell, he interjected, 'don't go there.' to which I replied, 'that's what I was going to say."[181] That is what the Clinton Clergy need to say. A hundred years from now, when all man's political achievements have passed into the sea of oblivion, this is all that will be of the least consequence.

Chapter Fifteen

IT IS NOT TOO LATE FOR CLINTON TO BE A GREAT MAN

Bill Clinton can change. There is still a way he can go down in history as one of the greatest presidents who ever lived. It is not too late for him to start all over. To do this, he must stop listening to his misleading ministers and accept what the Bible says is the cause and cure of his troubles.

On August 18, 1998, Rev. Philip Wogaman said that, in his view, the President apologized sufficiently, both to his family and the nation, in his...statement.[182] This apology is good and appropriate. But, while an apology is a step in the right direction, it does not go far enough to correct the President's problems.

Wogaman failed to address the real issue. Jesus Christ said the President's adultery was the results of a bad heart. The Scripture says: "The heart is deceitful above all things, and desperately wicked" (Jeremiah 17:9).

Dr. Robert Schuller shared the 51st Psalm with the President, who in turn quoted from it in the midst of his trouble. This Psalm pinpoints the origin of Mr. Clinton trouble: "Behold, I was shapen in iniquity; and in sin did my mother conceive me" (Psalm 51:5). The trouble is in the President's nature. He, like all men, was born with an evil nature—a passion for evil.

Clinton's Clergymen, as a group, ignore the root of man's problems—his wicked, depraved nature. Look at a cuddly, cute little baby. As much as we adore him, he is a self-centered little creature who screams and butts his head on the floor when he does not get what he wants. He demands instant gratification of every desire. He acts as if he is the center of the universe and never considers anyone else. This is the essence of evil and it is a problem we are all born with: "For from within, out of the heart of men, proceed evil thoughts, adulteries, fornications, murders, thefts, covetousness, wickedness, deceit, lasciviousness, an evil eye, blasphemy, pride, foolishness: All these evil things come from within, and defile the man" (Mark 7:21-23). As a minister of the Bible, Wogaman should be quick to recognize Mr. Clinton has something desperately wrong inside him that an apology will not solve. The problem is traceable right back to his birth: "Yea, in heart ye work wickedness....The wicked are estranged from the womb: they go astray as soon as they be born, speaking lies" (Psalm 58:2,3).

When President Clinton looked into the camera and told the American people a lie, it came from a heart that is corrupt. Jesus Christ said: "Either make the tree good, and his fruit good; or else make the tree corrupt, and his fruit corrupt: for the tree is known by his fruit. Oh generation of vipers, how can ye, being evil, speak good things? for out of the abundance of the heart the mouth speaketh. A good man out of the good treasure of the heart bringeth forth good things: and an evil man out of the evil treasure bringeth forth evil things" (Matthew 12:33-35).

All of the confessions and apologies the President can make will not change his conduct because they do not correct the evil nature he was born with.

COUNSELING IS NO SUBSTITUTE FOR CONVERSION

Rev. Shropshire, a minister in Clinton's Foundry United Methodist Church, said he experienced a *"deja vu"* to an earlier scandal, when Foundry's then-head minister confessed to a number of affairs with parishioners, and "when it came time to leave . . . also started to blame other people, and that's what I found troubling about President Clinton's statement." Shropshire said he hoped the President would seek psychological counseling to understand his own behavior, and figure out "why the most powerful man in the world is suddenly overcome by lust for a young woman."[183] Failing to understand the President's problem is not in his head but in his heart. This pastor suggests he sit down and talk with someone about the trouble. Regarding "counseling," the Bible does not award the title of "counselor" to any person but Jesus Christ: "For unto us a child is born, unto us a son is given: and the government shall be upon his shoulder: and his name shall be called Wonderful, Counselor" (Isaiah 9:6). This Counselor says, "Verily I say unto you, Except ye be converted, and become as little children, ye shall not enter into the kingdom of heaven" (Matthew 18:3).

If Bill Clinton talked with Jesus Christ, it would not be the kind of conversation he has had with his pastors. Jesus pulled no punches with prominent people. When He met the religious ruler named Nicodemus, a powerful, highly educated man who tithed, studied Scripture and attended church faithfully, Christ informed him, "Except a man be born again, he cannot see the kingdom of God" (John 3:3). The brilliant ruler asked, "How can a man be born when he is old? can he enter the second time into his mother's womb, and be born?" Jesus explained He wasn't talking about a natural birth, He was talking about but a spiritual birth: "Except a man be born of water and of the Spirit, he cannot enter into the kingdom of God. That which is born of the flesh is flesh; and that which is born of the Spirit is spirit. Marvel not that I said unto thee, Ye must be born again. The wind bloweth where it listeth, and thou hearest the sound thereof, but canst not tell whence it cometh, and whither it goeth: so is every one that is born of the Spirit" (John 3:4-8).

This spiritual birth takes the moral laws written in stone and imprints them in men's hearts: "But this shall be the covenant that I will make with the house of Israel; After those days, saith the LORD, I will put my law in their inward parts, and write it in their hearts; and will be their God, and they shall be my people" (Jeremiah 31:33).

This new birth offers President Clinton a miraculous power that would enable him to resist temptations to lie and be unfaithful to his wife. The prophet Ezekiel described the life-changing experience as a heart transplant in which a stony heart is replaced with a tender, fleshy heart: "A new heart also will I give you, and a new spirit will I put within you: and I will take away the stony heart out of your flesh, and I will give you an heart of flesh." This transplant results in a person keeping God's laws: "And I will put my spirit within you, and cause you to walk in my statutes, and ye shall keep my judgments, and do them" (Ezekiel 36:26,27). Righteousness is the natural result of this supernatural birth: "If ye know that he is righteous, ye know that every one that doeth righteousness is born of him" (I John 2:29).

WHAT AN IMPACT
A CONVERTED CLINTON COULD MAKE

Imagine the impact it would make on the world if President Clinton announced, "I have been born again. I have been a hypocrite, but now Jesus Christ has come into my heart and changed me into a new person. I have spent my life sitting in the church while living an immoral life. I want to start my new life by assuring the American people that, by the grace of God, you will not ever hear of Bill Clinton chasing skirts. Also, I want to make restitution. I pledge to my staff and friends, that I will work to raise money to pay off their legal bills which resulted from my long time cover-up. I want to apologize to Kenneth Starr, a Christian brother, for the way in which my staff and I have assassinated his character. I want to assure my enemies, who have worked to destroy me, that I forgive them. And most important, allow me to give this word of advice: "Do not believe all the nonsense my preachers have preached that is not in the Bible. Find a minister that preaches God's Word and listen to him."

A testimony like this, backed by a changed life, would rock the world. It could undo Clinton's bad influence. It could turn thousands away from their lying and adultery. It could lead many to Christ and impact the morals of our nation. Surely, he would go down in history as a uniquely honest and admirable man. This is what millions of Christians are praying will take place, and it is still not too late for it to happen.

Chapter Sixteen

RESETTING AMERICA'S MORAL COMPASS

Sometimes it takes quite a shocking defeat to awaken a nation to victory. America was sleeping its way through World War II until Japan hit Pearl Harbor and decimated her Pacific fleet. She could have easily chosen to give up and say, "They have destroyed our Pacific fleet. We will never recover from this. We can't win. We are whipped. The world changes. Democracy is an old fashion concept. We must learn to enjoy our new found freedom from responsibility. Let the Japanese worry with our responsibility from now on." But we didn't. Japan went too far when she blatantly attacked our Pacific command center, whipped our Navy and humiliated our nation. This devastating attack jarred America awake. Japan was a power that could no longer be ignored. America rose up to fight this tyrannical powers that had been raping the planet for years. Instead of giving up, America got up, retooled her factories, trained her troops, sacrificed her luxuries and whipped the most powerful, evil forces the world has ever witnessed. Out of the painful tragedy of Pearl Harbor victory was born.

Today, America is sleeping her way through a devastating attack on her values. This attack has decimated the American family, drugged her youth, overrun her prisons and now corrupted her government. She could easily choose to give up and say, "They have destroyed all our historic values. We will never recover from this. We can't win. We are whipped. The world changes. Morality is an old-fashioned concept. We must learn to enjoy our newfound freedom from the old rules. Let society worry about our moral irresponsibility from now on." But hopefully we won't. Perhaps sin went too far when it blatantly invaded our nation's sacred Oval Office, whipped our Commander-in-Chief and humiliated our nation. The devastating Clinton disaster could awaken America to see moral decay is a very real, dangerous enemy that cannot be ignored. She could rise up to fight the tyrannical evil that has been raping the nation's morals for years. Instead of giving up, America could wake up, and rise up, reestablish her morals, train her children in values, sacrifice her indulgences and whip the most powerful, evil assault on moral values the world has ever witnessed. Hopefully, out of the painful experience of the Clinton tragedy, victory will be born.

AMERICA NEEDS TO RESET
HER MORAL COMPASS

Bill Clinton isn't the only one who needs to repent. America's leaders—in government, the media, schools and entertainment—need to repent of allowing our nation's moral drift. The approval ratings of a lying President with an adolescent sense of sexual appropriateness are amazingly high. The public display of cynicism about a man assaulting our children's moral values is shocking. If we are to believe the polls, the majority of our people do not even care about honesty and character. A sexual revolution that began with topless shoe-shine girls on San Francisco's North Beach has ended with a bottomless President in the nation's White House. America's giggling over the Clinton girls is sobering. Americans have slept through the most radical cultural revolution in history. Now we are getting a loud, alarming, wake-up call.

Stephen L. Carter, the Yale law professor who wrote *"Civility: Manners, Morals, and the Etiquette of Democracy,"* says, "Sometimes it takes a rude shock to wake the national conscience, which is, in our post-modern era, not defeated but exhausted. That conscience needs awakening because our sense of right and wrong is ultimately what makes America a special place." Carter, writing in *The New York Times*, declared, "This depressing scandal might represent our best chance at reinvigorating our shared belief in an American moral code—the clear understanding of right and wrong....A moral code for which we are prepared to sacrifice our own short-term interests, in exchange for the nation's long-term good.... In its place we have set an ethic of selfishness, in which sacrifice is a dirty word, in which successful leadership is measured only by the rise of the S. & P. 500 and in which the only use of words like right and wrong is for political gain."

If we are to save our children from the new, monstrous influence of dishonesty and deviance, we must wake up and fight for the values that will grow them into men and women of character. If we are to save our families from the mindless betrayal of adultery, we must wake up and fight for the values that will steady our homes through the rough seas of temptation. If we are to save our nation from the self-centered, pleasure-seeking that abandons all concern for our fellow citizens, we must wake up and fight for the self-sacrificing concern that held us together while we struggled to build this nation.

THE CHURCH NEEDS TO REPENT
OF ITS SINFUL SILENCE

Rev. Richard Cizik, the interim Washington director of the National Association of Evangelicals, says the Clinton scandal suggests a failure on the part of religious leaders, "Why has the church not been able to nurture, discipline, and train one of her own (Clinton, a lifelong Southern Baptist) for responsible leadership in civil society?" he declared. "It's a question that should not go unanswered—and means that this crisis could be viewed as God's wake-up call to the church, as much as to Bill Clinton or the Congress."[184]

Bill Clinton is not the only one who needs to repent. The Christian Church needs to repent. Even more shocking than the apathy of America about the President's sins is the cynicism of the church. There is an appalling silence. There is no loud united cry for repentance from the churches of our land. There is no clear trumpet sounding the way out of temptation. In a time of historic opportunity to show mankind its need for the power of Jesus Christ to strength them against temptation, all we hear is, "don't cast the first stone." Heaven is surely crying over the church's unconcern for the soul of a sinner.

The true Christians of America need to rise up and expel the traitors in the pulpits of this country. Men like the Clinton Clergy, who have told the President the Bible is not true and repentance of sin is not necessary, should immediately be put out of our pulpits. No other army in history has allowed traitors to train its troops. If the Bible is not an authentic guide from heaven, we should close our churches and forget Christianity. If it is, we need to demand it be preached from our pulpits.

People who really believe in Christ need to begin restoring fallen members. When a fellow member of the church sins, he needs rebuke, prayer and restoration. If that fails he must be removed from the membership to awaken him to his rebellious condition and gain his repentance. The time has come for the church to get serious about following Jesus Christ, who came to "save" men from sin, not to establish social clubs.

Repentance, like judgment, must begin among those in God's house: "For the time is come that judgment must begin at the house of God: and if it first begin at us, what shall the end be of them that obey not the gospel of God? And if the righteous scarcely be saved, where shall the ungodly and the sinner appear?" (I Peter 4:17,18).

WE THE PEOPLE NEED TO REPENT
OF OUR PERSONAL SINS

Bill Clinton is not the only one who needs to repent. We the people, every one of us, need to get on our faces before God and repent. The moral defeat of our President shows us how vulnerable we are to attacks from the enemy of evil. It does not matter how educated, how skilled, or how determined we are, without the power of Jesus Christ we are vulnerable to falling. To have this victorious power demands that we re-pent—be willing to abandon every sin, no matter how pleasur-able and trust our lives, our souls, our all, into the hands of the Lord Jesus Christ. Church membership, Bible memorization, church attendance, public prayer are not enough. Clinton showed us this. We must repent and be genuinely converted if we are to stand against the enemies of our soul.

The most shocking thing about the President's moral fall has not been the blatant, repetitious way in which he has violated propriety. It has been the way the people, understanding the situation, have loved having it so. As the prophet Jeremiah complained about Judah, amidst their prosperity they had "a rebellious heart....Among my people are found wicked men....The prophets prophesy falsely...and my people love to have it so" (Jeremiah 5:23,26,31). Prosperous America is in the same condition. Preachers are preaching falsely and the people to have it so. This moral indifference demands repentance as much as Clinton's lying and adultery does.

It may be, as William J. Bennett says, "that we have lost our national capacity for moral outrage—at least as long as the economy is humming along. Even if the current scandal had never arisen, our moral sense has been corroded by the steady drip-drip-drip of everyday lying and cheating."

Jarred by the victorious attack of evil on our President, America could be getting her last call to reset her moral compass.

END NOTES

CHAPTER 1

[1] Dee Dee Meyers, *Time*, August 31, 1998, p. 40.

[2] AP, May 18, 1995.

[3] Dr. Jerome Levin, *The Clinton Syndrome*, (Prima Publishing, Rocklin, CA) pp. 101,102.

[4] Paul Fink, *The Dysfunctional President*, (Secaucus, N.J., Carol Publishing Group) p.132.

[5] Paul Fink, *The Dysfunctional President*, (Secaucus, N.J., Carol Publishing Group) p.221.

[6] Dr. Jerome Levin, *The Clinton Syndrome*, (Prima Publishing, Rocklin, CA) p. 12.

[7] Paul G. Labadie, *USA Today*, October 14, 1998, p. 15A.

[8] *USA Today*, October 14, 1998, p. 15A.

[9] Julia Malone, *Atlanta Constitution Journal*, Friday, March 6, 1998.

[10] Dorothy Rabinowitz, *The Wall Street Journal*, September 18, 1998, p. W13.

[11] George Melloan, *The Wall Street Journal*, September 15, 1998, p. A23.

[12] David Maraniss, *The Clinton Enigma*, (New York, N.Y., Simon & Schuster) pp. 101, 102.

[13] Billy Graham, Interview by Katie Couric, Today Show, March 5, 1998.

[14] Jeremy, on the *Acts\Odyssey network*, Aug. 23, 1998.

[15] David Maraniss, *First in His Class*, (New York, N.Y., Simon & Schuster) p. 464.

[16] David Maraniss, *First in His Class*, (New York, N.Y., Simon & Schuster), p. 424.

[17] David Maraniss, *First in His Class*, (New York, N.Y., Simon & Schuster), p. 435.

[18] David Maraniss, *First in His Class*, (New York, N.Y., Simon & Schuster) pp. 434, 435.

[19] David Maraniss, *First in His Class*, (New York, N.Y., Simon & Schuster), p. 435.

[20] David Maraniss, *The Clinton Enigma*, (New York, N.Y., Simon & Schuster) pp. 101, 102.

[21] David Maraniss, *First in His Class*, (New York: Simon & Schuster, 1996), p. 451.

[22] *Time*, August 31, 1998, p. 29.

CHAPTER 2

[23] David Klinghoffer, *The Wall Street Journal*, January 3, 1997.

[24] Joseph Parker, *The People's Bible*, vol. 15, (London: Hodder and Stoughton, 1900) p. 282.

[25] Warren W. Wiersbe, *The Integrity Crisis*, (Nashville, Oliver Nelson, 1988) p.19.

[26] Adele M. Stan, *Mother Jones*, December 1995.

[27] Warren W. Wiersbe, *The Integrity Crisis*, (Nashville, Oliver Nelson, 1988) p.19.

[28] Jerry Falwell, *25 of the Greatest Sermons Ever Preached*, (Grand Rapids: Baker Book House, 1983), p. 18.

[29] David Klinghoffer, *The Wall Street Journal*, January 3, 1997.

[30] Adelle M. Banks, *Religious News Service*, August 29, 1998.

[31] Larry E. Ball, *World*, September 26, 1988, p. 4.

[32] Cal Thomas, *Newsday*, March 10, 1998.

[33] David Maraniss, *First in His Class*, (New York: Simon & Schuster, 1996), pp. 57, 58.

[34] Billy Graham, the *NBC Today Show*, March 5, 1998.

CHAPTER 3

[35] W. O. Vaught, *Believe Plus Nothing*, (1983), p. 17.

[36] W. O. Vaught, *Believe Plus Nothing,* (1983), p. 18.

[37] W. O. Vaught, *Believe Plus Nothing,* (1983), p. 18.

[38] W. O. Vaught, *Believe Plus Nothing,* (1983), p. 18.

[39] Albert Brumley, *Victory in Jesus.*

[40] W. O. Vaught, *Believe Plus Nothing,* (1983), p. 22.

[41] W. O. Vaught, *Believe Plus Nothing,* (1983), p. 11.

[42] Joseph Henry Thayer, *Greek-English Lexicon of the New Testament,* (Grand Rapids: Zondervan, 1962), p. 406.

[43] D. Martyn Lloyd-Jones, *Studies in the Sermon on the Mount* (Grand Rapids: Eerdmans, 1959), 2:248.

[44] W. O. Vaught, *Believe Plus Nothing* (1983), pp. 18,19.

[45] *The Washington Post,* January 20, 1997, Final Edition.

[46] H.A. Ironside, *Except Ye Repent,* (Grand Rapids: Zondervan, 1937), p. 11.

[47] Cal Thomas, Editorial, September 15, 1998.

[48] Charles H. Spurgeon, *The Soul Winner,* (Pasadena, Texas: Pilgrim, 1978), pp. 32 33.

[49] James Stewart, *Evangelism,* (Revival Literature, Philadelphia, Pa.) pp.41,42.

[50] James Stewart, *Evangelism,* (Revival Literature, Philadelphia, Pa.) pp.22.

[51] H.A. Ironside, *Except Ye Repent,* (Grand Rapids: Zondervan, 1937), p. 10.

CHAPTER 4

[52] Jill Lawrence, *USA Today,* August 20, 1998, p. 6A.

[53] Stanley A. Renshon, *High Hopes,* (New York, Routledge), p. IX.

[54] *St. Petersburg Times,* quoted in *U.S. News & World Report,* August 31, 1998, p. 32.

[55] By Tamala M. Edwards, and Romesh Rathesat, *Time,* August 31, 1998, p.41.

[56] Stanley A. Renshon, *High Hopes,* (New York, Routledge), p. IX.

[57] Stanley A. Renshon, *High Hopes,* (New York, Routledge), p. XV.

[58] Scrapbook, "Clinton's Pentagon Papers," *The Weekly Standard,* June 15, 1998.

[59] Robert A. Manning and James Presystup, *The Wall Street Journal,* June 25, 1998, p. A22.

[60] Ann H. Coulter , *High Crimes and Misdemeanors,* (Washington, D. C.,

Regency Publishing, Inc., p. 39.

[61] Charles Krauthammer, *Time*, September 28, 1998, p. 102.

[62] Dee Dee Myers,, *Time,* August 31, 1998, p. 40.

[63] Ann H. Coulter, *High Crimes and Misdemeanors*, (Washington, D. C., Regency Publishing, Inc.), pp. 307,308

[64] *U.S. News & World Report*, August 31, 1998.

[65] *Atlanta Constitution Journal*, September 11, 1998, p. 16.

[66] William J. Bennett, *The Wall Street Journal*, November 10, 1998, p. A22.

[67] Bob Woodward and Carl Bernstein, "The Final Days Part Two," *Newsweek*, April 12, 1976.

[68] Ann H. Coulter, *High Crimes and Misdemeanors*, (Washington, D. C., Regency Publishing, Ine.), p. 16.

[69] Ann H. Coulter, *High Crimes and Misdemeanors*, (Washington, D. C., Regency Publishing, Inc.), p. 306.

[70] Ann H. Coulter, *High Crimes and Misdemeanors*, (Washington, D. C., Regency Publishing, Inc.), p. 11.

[71] Ann H. Coulter, *High Crimes and Misdemeanors*, (Washington, D. C., Regency Publishing, Inc.), p. 14.

[72] Cal Thomas, *Los Angeles Times*, August 17, 1998.

[73] Ann H. Coulter, *High Crimes and Misdemeanors*, (Washington, D. C., Regency Publishing, Inc.), p. 14.

[74] Cal Thomas, *The Los Angeles Time,* August 17, 1998.

CHAPTER 5

[75] Ann H. Coulter, *High Crimes and Misdemeanors*, (Washington, D. C., Regency Publishing, Inc.), p. 44.

[76] James Carville, *And the Horse He Rode In On*, (Simon & Schuster, New York, 1998), p. 107.

[77] William Bennett, *The Death of Outrage*, (Free Press, New York, 1998.), p. 22.

[78] Jill Lawrence, *USA Today*, August 20, 1998.

[79] Jill Lawrence, *USA Today*, August 20, 1998.

[80] William J. Bennett, *The Death of Outrage,* (Free Press, New York, 1998).

[81] William Bennett , *The Death of Outrage*, (Free Press, New York, 1998), p. 22

[82] Cal Thomas, "Billy Graham Should Remember The White House Is Not in Heaven," syndicated column March 10, 1998.

[83] Philip Wogaman, *The Jerusalem Post*, daily Internet edition, August 18, 1998.

[84] Hanna Rosin, *The Washington Post*, August 19, 1998; p. A17.

[85] Dr. Jerome Levin, *The Clinton Syndrome*, (Prima Publishing, Rocklin, CA) p. 80.

[86] Dr. Paul Fick, *The Dysfunctional President*, (Carol Publishing Group, Secaucus, N.J.) pp.126,127.

[87] Ibid., p.127.

[88] Raouel Berger, *Impeachment: The Constitutional Problems*, 211 and 201 (1973) (quoting 8 Howell 197,200, Art. 8).

[89] Ann H. Coulter , *High Crimes and Misdemeanors*, (Washington, D. C., Regency Publishing, Inc.), p. 19.

[90] J. Budziszewske, *World*, September 26, 1998, p.21.

[91] Dr. Jerome Levin, *The Clinton Syndrome*, (Prima Publishing, Rocklin, CA) p.129.

[92] Dr. Jerome Levin, *The Clinton Syndrome*, (Prima Publishing, Rocklin, CA) p. 158.

[93] Andy Rooney, syndicated column, September 25, 1998.

[94] Andy Rooney, syndicated column, September 25, 1998.

[95] Cal Thomas, *World*, September 26, 1998, p. 9.

CHAPTER 6

[96] *Time*, August 31, 1998, p.30.

[97] Julia Malone, *Atlanta Constitution Journal*, March 6, 1998.

[98] Word number 2919 in *Strong's Greek & Hebrew Dictionary*

CHAPTER 7

[99] *National Council of Churches News*, September 12, 1998.

[100] *Larry King Show*, September 24, 1998.

[101] Dr. Jerome Levin, *The Clinton Syndrome*, (Prima Publishing, Rocklin, CA) p.167.

[102] Mark Tooley, *Heterodoxy*, October, 1997.

[103] *AP*, Saturday, March 14, 1998.

[104] David Klinghoffer, *The Wall Street Journal*, January 3, 1997.

[105] Mark Tooley, *Heterodoxy*, October, 1997.

[106] Mark Tooley, *Heterodoxy*, October, 1997.

[107] Cal Thomas, newspaper column, April 21, 1995.

[108] Barna Research Group, *Biblical Recorder*, October 10, 1998, p. 12.

[109] Ann Coulter, *High Crimes and Misdemeanors*, p. 10.

[110] *Strong's Greek and Hebrew Dictionary* numbers 730, 733 and
        2845,5449, 5453.
[111] Family Research Institute, P.O. Box 2091, Washington, D.C. 20013.

CHAPTER 8
[112] Cal Thomas, Editorial, September 9, 1998.
[113] *USA Today*, September 14, 1998, p. 6D.
[114] J. Oliver Buswell, Jr., *Ten Reasons Why a Christian Does not Live a
        Wicked Life*, p. 16.
[115] J. Oliver Buswell, Jr., *Ten Reasons Why a Christian Does not Live a
        Wicked Life*, p. 26.
[116] J. Oliver Buswell, Jr., *Ten Reasons Why a Christian Does not Live a
        Wicked Life*, p. 32.
[117] J. Oliver Buswell, Jr., *Ten Reasons Why a Christian Does not Live a
        Wicked Life*, p. 33.
[118] J. Oliver Buswell, Jr., *Ten Reasons Why a Christian Does not Live a
        Wicked Life*, pp. 33,34.
[119] W. O. Vaught, *God's Calendar*, (1984) p. 87.

CHAPTER 9
[120] Mark Tooley, *Heterodoxy*, October 1997, p. 11.
[121] J. Philip Wogaman, *Speaking the Truth in Love*, (Louisville, KY,
        Westminster John Know Press), p. 199.
[122] J. Philip Wogaman, *Speaking the Truth in Love*, (Louisville, KY,
        Westminster John Know Press), p. 198.
[123] J. Philip Wogaman, *Speaking the Truth in Love*, (Louisville, KY,
Westminster John Know Press), p. 41.
[124] J. Philip Wogaman, *Speaking the Truth in Love*, (Louisville, KY,
        Westminster John Know Press), p. 86.
[125] Maureen Dowd, *New York Times News Service*.

CHAPTER 10
[126] Chuck Colson, *Larry King Live*, September 2, 1998.
[127] Chuck Colson, *Larry King Live*, September 2, 1998.
[128] David Maraniss, *The Clinton Enigma*, (Simon & Schuster, New York,
        1998), p.17.
[129] *The New York Times*, quoted in *U.S. News & World Report*, August 31,
        1998, p. 32.

[130] Anchorage Times, quoted in *U.S. News & World Report*, August 31, 1998.

[131] Laura Schlessinger, *Religion News Service*, September 26, 1998.

[132] Laura Schlessinger, *Religion News Service*, September 26, 1998.

[133] Dale Hanson Bourke, *Religion News Service*, September 26, 1998.

[134] Wes Pruden, *Current Thoughts and Trends*, August, 1998.

CHAPTER 11

[135] *Religion News Service*, August 29, 1998.

[136] *Religious News Service*, August 29, 1998.

[137] *Baptist Message*, October 29, 1998, p. 2.

[138] *USA Weekend*, November 13-15, 1998, p.2.

[139] *Religious News Service*, August 29, 1998.

[140] *Religious News Service*, August 29, 1998.

CHAPTER 12

[141] Dorothy Rabinowitz, *The Wall Street Journal*, September 18, 1998, p. W13.

[142] Billy Graham, interview by Katie Couric, *Today Show*, March 5, 1998.

[143] Cal Thomas, *Newsday* (ND), March 10, 1998.

[144] Chuch Baldwin, *"Chuck Baldwin Live,"* posted on the Internet September 2, 1998.

[145] Julia Malone, *Atlanta Constitution*, Friday, March 6, 1998.

[146] AP, January 27, 1998.

[147] AP, January 27, 1998.

[148] AP, January 27, 1998.

[149] George F. Will, Baton Rouge, La. *The Advocate*, December 17, 1998, p. 9B.

[150] J. Budziszewske, *World*, September 26, 1998, p.21.

[151] George Stroup, *The Atlanta Journal*, September 26, 1998, p. D1.

[152] Bill Clinton, *The Atlanta Journal*, September 26, 1998, p. D1.

[153] Steven Lebow, *The Atlanta Journal*, September 26, 1998, p D1.

[154] *USA Today*, November 16, 1998, p. 15A.

[155] Cal Thomas, *Athens Newspapers Inc.*, posted on the Internet on August 28 1998.

[156] *The Atlanta Journal*, September 26, 1998, p D1.

[157] Max Lucado, *The Atlanta Journal*, September 26, 1998, p. D1.

[158] Franklin Graham, *The Charlotte Observer*, September 11, 1998, p. 12A.

[159] *The Wall Street Journal*, September 18, 1998, p. W13.

CHAPTER 13
[160] W. O. Vaught, *Believe Plus Nothing*, p. 16.
[161] R. Albert Mohler, *World*, August 8, 1998, p.19.
[162] J. Philip Wogaman, *Speaking the Truth in Love*, (Louisville, KY, Westminster John Know Press), p. 199.
[163] Hour of Power, May 31/June 8, 1997. Published in *Foundation Magazine*, May-June 1997.
    and in England's *Sword & Trowel*, 1997, no.3, p.31.
[164] Billy Graham, *The Challenge*, (New York, Pocket Books), pp. 58,59.
[165] Katie Couric interview, the *NBC* Today Show, March 5, 1998.
[166] W. O. Vaught, *Believe Plus Nothing*, p. 26.

CHAPTER 14
[167] James Carville, *And the Horse He Rode In On*, (Simon & Schuster, New York), p. 115.
[168] James Carville, *And the Horse He Rode In On*, (Simon & Schuster, New York), p. 115, 116.
[169] James Carville, *And the Horse He Rode In On*, (Simon & Schuster, New York), p. 115.
[170] William R. Mattox, Jr., *USA Today*, October 29, 1998, p. 15A.
[171] William R. Mattox, Jr., *USA Today*, October 29, 1998, p. 15A.
[172] Cal Thomas, Baton Rouge *Morning Advocate*, September 15, 1998.
[173] Jerry Walls, *USA Today*, October 29, 1998, p. 15A.
[174] John Patten, *USA Today*, October 29, 1998, p. 15A.
[175] David Maraniss, *The Clinton Enigma*, (Simon & Schuster, New York, 1998), p. 42.
[176] David Maraniss, *The Clinton Enigma*, (Simon & Schuster, New York, 1998), p. 110.
[177] AP January 21, 1996.
[178] Billy Graham, *The Challenge*, (Pocket Books, New York), pp. 57,58.
[179] Billy Graham, *The Challenge*, (Pocket Books, New York), pp. 57.
[180] James A. Stewart, *Evangelism*, (Revival Literature, Philadelphia, Pa.) p. 17.
[181] James A. Stewart, *Evangelism*, (Revival Literature, Philadelphia, Pa.) p. 17.
[182] William R. Mattox, Jr., *USA Today*, October 29, 1998, p. 15A.

CHAPTER 15

[183] Hanna Rosin, *The Washington Post*, August 19, 1998, p. A17.

[184] Religious News Service, December 26, 1998